The Enlightened
Party Manifesto
(Its Principles &
Ideologies)

Published By CreateSpace
4900 Lacross Road,
North Charleston, SC, 29406
ISBN 978-1533023452

Printed in the United States of America.

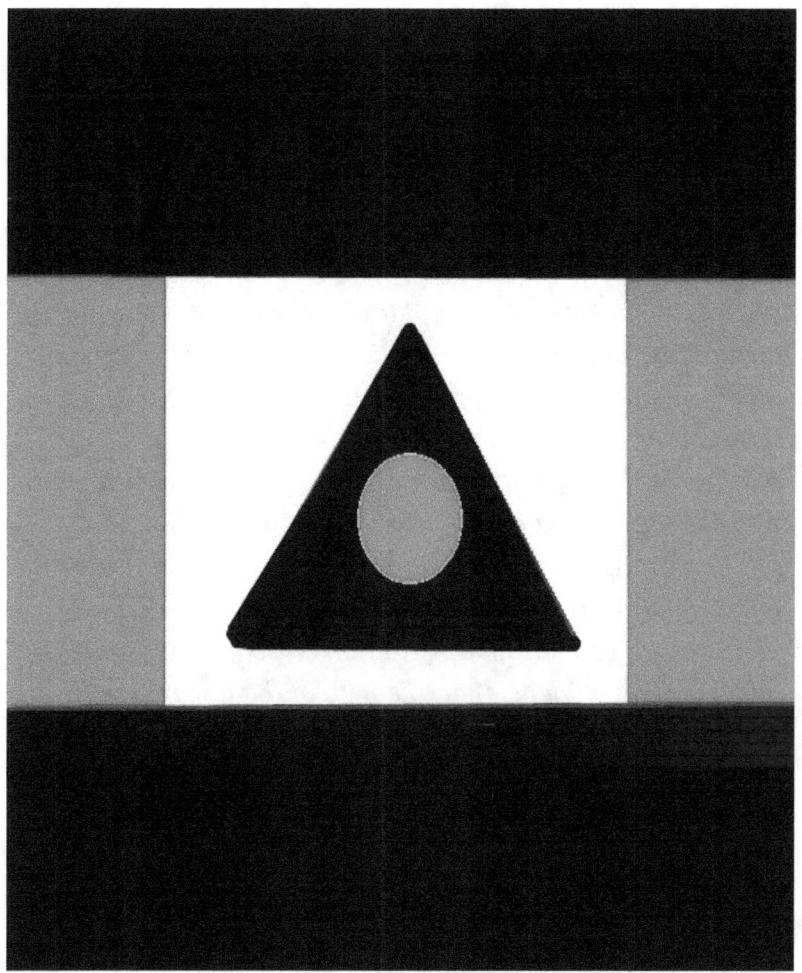

*-The official flag & insignia of The Enlightened Party;
designed and adopted by its founder, Simon Mark Alvarez-*

*-The science of the Law of Attraction to be taught and
instructed to all students by instructors in all educational
institutions in the United States of America, public or
private-*

*The Enlightened Party is a political party that is founded
upon the principles & ideology of freedom, liberty,
prosperity, humanitarian-aid towards mankind, security,
tranquility, and supports civil liberties and civil rights for
all races, ethnicities, genders, and people of sexual
orientation. Equality and fairness is what represents the
platform for this political party. Biasness, favoritism, and
corruption contradicts the exact opposite of what this
political party stands for and represents. The Enlightened
Party encourages, advocates, and will always defend the
idea that all educational institutions instruct and educate
all American students the "theory" of the law of attraction;
that is recognized by scientists but not yet recognized by
any government in the world. The definition of
Enlightenment is defined as:*

*"The state of having knowledge or understanding: the act
of giving someone knowledge or understanding." - The
definition of enlightenment.*

*The 21st century is a new age of unlimited information that
is guaranteed to be found based upon an individual's
research; as well as that individual's desire, persistence,*

4

and belief that those questions that he or she seeks, will be delivered with an appropriate answer. It is no longer a secret that all things, events, and/or circumstances that are delivered into a person's is based upon the images that appear in that individual's brain, and also emotions of what that person felt prior to experiencing the event or circumstance. What does this mean? This means that the human-brain is severely powerful, sensitive, and the sole creator of everything that is carefully manifested into something physical based upon an image in the brain and an emotion. In a way, this would and can imply that human-beings are characterized as being the "God" that is publicly mentioned in religious-books (such as the Holy Bible & the Holy Quran) and who people worship when they seek comfort, praise and/or perfection. It's no longer a secret that the human-brain consists of energy; thus a thought consists of energy, and since the world and Universe is made entirely of energy, we share ourselves within this same energy; thus there is no plausible way or method to conceal our true desires and emotions from the world and the Universe. Since the world and Universe knows what every thought in the human brain is being transpired and transmitted (like an invisible signal) to the Universe and the world; as if the world and Universe are us (which we are all the same), there is no doubt that every human-being on Earth, has the capability to become and attract anything that he or she is thinking about and desires.

5

*Scientists attracted other scientists to make discoveries of
something beneficial, essential, and/or controversial based
upon one scientist's desire to seek and go on a quest for an
answer to something that has always had a question
waiting to be answered. These scientists attracted each
other, no matter how far apart in the world they were to
each other. This is one of many examples that I can put
forth. But this is a book based on the principles &
ideologies of the Enlightened Party; and not on the law of
attraction. The law of attraction does exists as the law of
gravity exists; as well as the law of love. The only problem
is that young children that elevate to teenagers, and then to
young adults, and then finally adults, are never taught in
educational institutions that the law of attraction exists;
and more importantly, that their (the people) minds consist
of energy that is powerful enough to attract and receive
relevant people, circumstances, and/or events based upon
those thoughts. If educational facilities educated students
on the grave dangers of feeling bad and doing harm to
others will only attract that same circumstances (into their
lives), based upon the energy and actions that have been
manifested; which were initially created from that person's
brain, then, students who prepare for their future lives may
consider doing righteous and compassionate actions
towards their fellow human-beings and all living things.
The key-point is to aid & guide our world for the better;
while always protecting it from evil people who desire to*

*taint it with unfair and terrible actions. Wealthy will always
attract more wealth and luxury, and poverty will always
attract more poverty and that is why they are separated. If
students are educated to do compassionate and caring
things for others and the world, otherwise, face the
inevitable consequences of receiving negative events,
people, and circumstance into the future, then crime would
be significantly reduced. Fear would play a factor into the
student's mind as they know that every thought that is
transpired into their mind is preparing to manifest
whatever their image and emotions is currently within them.
The result can either be good or bad; or perhaps a blessing
in disguise (bad at first, but good in the end). The ultimate
purpose, reason, and justification for this political party to
demand the federal government to sign-into-law the very
same bill the founder of the Enlightened Party authored, is
to benefit millions of Americans to convince themselves that
innovations and possibilities are possible to accomplish
and establish based upon an individual's mentality, desire,
and emotions. The results can either deliver wealth or
poverty or something in between; in the end, the decision is
made up to them. The warning is only made available to the
students, the responsibility is up to the student to make
their ultimate decisions. Millions of Americans understand
the law of gravity, of where everything on Earth must
remain on the ground until sufficient strength is engaged in
order to transport something heavy. Even a child*

understands the fact when something is either too heavy for them to lift. However, millions and millions of intelligent and articulate Americans do not know or understand the law of attraction. They have never even heard of it. The fact is, is that it has been preserved throughout history by wealthy and powerful figures in society that have suppressed it from regular minorities (their average citizens). I can never say that any human-being is a minority. I only mention minority because that's what was the mentality of these powerful figures, believing that they're superiority demanded the automatic right to know the secrets of the Universe against the minority (the inferior people). However, superiority and inferiority are theories; invented by a selfish and immoral powerful-figure to convince other wealthy elites to keep this secret amongst themselves. If millions and millions of Americans understood the law of attraction, and what it can bring to that person's life, the abundance, the magic, the prosperity, the many innovations and dreams, then more people would begin consciously practicing it then subconsciously practicing it. The truth of the matter is that over seven billion people on Earth (the estimated world population) subconsciously (never knowing or realizing) practice the law of attraction into their lives and do not realize it. It is crucial, essential, and important for every human-being in America to know, understand, and comprehend, that all current and future events are manifested and put into place

*based upon that person's thoughts and emotions. It is a
duty and obligation for the United States federal
government to intervene in this matter; and thus establish
the proper statutes that require all elementary, middle, and
high school students to learn and understand on how the
law of attraction works; regardless, if it offends an
individual's religion, or it offends the parents of the
students religion; as it may but is not intended to offend in
any way; as the law of attraction is a natural automatic
system that operates twenty-four hours a day in every
single human-beings head. If a student can learn and
understand how to use it to their advantage, innovative
ideas are guaranteed to be established. More discoveries
and inventions can and inevitably happen because of one's
eagerness to desire to bring a new innovation in the world,
which will guarantee to attract the right resources and the
right people for the job. To burden Americans with the
scientific concept of the law of attraction, is to condone yet
another system of slavery. Liberating the mind with
negative and unwanted feelings, thoughts, and emotions is
the way to free mankind. Let the United States of America
be the first country to begin educating its people through
the educational system, the law of attraction to ensure that
Americans are given the magic formula for which every
human-being on Earth contain within themselves; but do
not understand its practice or power. and the only way for
Americans to understand this power is to be educated*

about it. No longer shall the privileged elite enjoy this practicing formula while the majority of the population are unknown to its absolute power because of suppression which has been apparent for centuries. If politicians in Congress support freedom and true emancipation, and the idea for the United States of America to be a superior nation above all nation

-Interest-Free Currency-

There is only one U.S. President in American history who issued an interest-free currency for the purpose of paying off all national debt; at least for the time being during the American civil war, which without its essential measure, the Union may have destroyed itself during or after the war with the Confederacy due to Bankruptsy. As Abraham Lincoln once said to the American people upon establishing his interest-free currency to the American people.

"The government should create, issue, and circulate all the currency and credit needed to satisfy the spending power of the government and the buying power of consumers. The privilege of creating and issuing money is not only the supreme prerogative of government, but it is the government's greatest creative opportunity. By the adoption of these principles, the long-felt want for a uniform medium will be satisfied. The taxpayers will be saved immense sums of interest, discounts, and exchanges.

The financing of all public enterprises, the maintenance of stable government and ordered progress, and the conduct of the Treasury will become matters of practical administration. The people can and will be furnished with a currency as safe as their own government. Money will cease to be the master and become the servant of humanity. Democracy will rise superior to the money power." - President Abraham Lincoln

It's generally not taught in public and private educational institutions to students on how our economy operates within our country; unless of course, students begin to take economic courses on their own free-will while attending college. Perhaps, there is a reason for that. Abraham Lincoln needed appropriate monetary funds to fund the civil war that he was engaged in against the Confederacy. Instead, of receiving a ridiculous loan with 36% interest from various banking institutions, he declined their ruthless offer, because he knew that if he accepted their offer, economic disaster (through severe debt) was inevitable for the United States. There would be no way to pay back all the money that was lent to the U.S government by the greedy bankers. Abraham Lincoln knew this; and summoned in a great friend of his (Colonel Dick Taylor), and till this very day, credited with reminding Abraham Lincoln of the Constitutional power, obligation, and authority the Congress of the United States has to oversee monetary policies for the nation.

11

*"Just get Congress to pass a bill authorizing the printing of
full legal tender treasury notes; and pay your soldiers with
them and go ahead and win your war with them also. If you
make them full legal tender, they will have the full section
of the government and be just as good as any money; as
Congress is given the express right by the Constitution." -
Colonel Dick Taylor*

*"As Congress is given the express right by the
Constitution." It is true, it's no lie or theory; if a person
decided to read the U.S Constitution; particularly Article 1,
section 8 & 10, which states that Congress has the power to:*

*"To coin money, regulate the value thereof, and of foreign
coin; and fix the standards of weights and measures." -
Article 1, Section 8*

&

*"Make anything but gold and silver coin a tender in
payment of debts." - Article 1, section 10*

**Before I proceed to demonstrate the dangers of borrowing
money from a central bank, whose sole purpose is to
strangle & enslave the economy of its borrowing nation to
death, through the burden of debt, (like the Federal
Reserve System), I must mention this last reference towards
the "Greenbacks," which even Great Britain recognized**

during the American civil war, was prosperous to the people, but dangerous for the lending-institutions.

"If this mischievous financial policy, which has its origin in North America, shall become edurated (hard) down to a fixture, then that governnment will furnish its own money without cost. It will pay off debts and be without debt. It will have all the money necessary to carry on its commerce. It will become prosperous without precedent in the history of the world. The brains, and wealth of all countries will go to North America. That country must be destroyed or it will destroy every monarchy on the globe." Hazard Circular - London Times

Clearly, the London times accepted the "Greenback Measure," as absolutely beneficial towards the American people. In politics, when a bill, measure, or innovation is debated, supported, or opposed, almost always the opposition involved condemning the idea or bill or measure. Whoever authored the article for the London Times, recognized its benefits towards the American people, but still condemned it because it opposed powerful interests who still desire to this very day to maintain their domination over all economies, in all nations. These ruthless bankers must be suppressed and stopped; as well as their allies. Therefore, the alternative or offensive approach to preventing their tyranny to extending any further, would be for a member of The Enlightened Party

(perhaps the founder of the newly-established party) to introduce a bill to Congress that contains the following three requirements.

1. *The United States Treasury will begin issuing interest-free "United States of America Notes" that is legal tender, both public and private. This new currency will be printed directly from the U.S Treasury and will not receive any assistance or aid in printing from the privately-owned Federal Reserve Bank. The United States Treasury will begin issuing this interest-free currency and begin the process of converting Federal Reserve Notes to United States of America Notes." The U.S government will have up to sixteen months to successfully complete the transition & value from the Federal Reserve Notes to the "United States of America Notes."*

2. *Federal Reserve Notes will be null and void; and declared worthless to pay off all debts public and private. Federal Reserve Notes will only contain value in terms of a "collectable-piece-of-history," which can be purchased from a collector but not converted to the "United States of America Notes."*

3. *The speedy & gradual process of abolishing the Federal Reserve System and the Internal Revenue Service permanently.*

14

The purpose of the interest-free currency to established is to ensure the safety of the America's interests by avoiding useless and unnecessary debts among its own citizens; thus removing the burden of debt, will be the same as freeing an enslaved American who is dominated by debt. The United States cannot succeed and be powerful above all nations with a burden of debt. As of the writing of this book, the United States of America is currently at 19 trillion dollars in U.S debt. That is a danger due to our country and civil liberties for all Americans; as the threat of hyperinflation and devaluation of the Federal Reserve Notes is critical, likely, and very possible. The Enlightened Party cannot support this reckless and abusive authority that is given to the banks by the federal government. The only way to prevent this tyranny from proceeding, and to ensure the domestic tranquility of our nation, is to do one of two things, or perhaps both things; if necessary:

1. *Elect a member of The Enlightened Party to the U.S Congress, as either a Congressman or Senator...*
2. *Overthrow the current U.S. Government which condone and protect this ruthless violation of our great nations conduct.*

To further demonstrate previous warnings from former U.S

Presidents (including a founding father), that explain and warn of the dangers of a central bank, this alone should encourage all Americans to accept and understand that central banks (the Federal Reserve System) are dangerous and a threat to every American in the United States. They are no friends or allies to the American people as you will see for yourself of warnings from people who lived to tell their experience with central banks while in office.

"If the American people ever allow private banks (the Federal Reserve System) to control the issue of their currency, first by inflation, then by deflation, the banks and corporations that will grow up around them will deprive the people of all property until their children wake up and homeless on the continent their fathers conquered. I believe that banking institutions are more dangerous to our liberties than standing armies. The issuing power should be taken from the banks and restored to the people, to whom it properly belongs." - President Thomas Jefferson

Going back to President Abraham Lincoln, and his liberating currency, the "Greenbacks," even he acknowledged his most true and ruthless enemy when he said:

"I have two great enemies! The southern Army in front of me and the financial institutions (the banks) in the rear. Of the two, the one in the rear is the greatest enemy. I see in

16

the future a crisis approaching that unnerves me and causes me to tremble for the safety of my country. As a result of the war, corporations have been enthroned and an era of corruption in high places will follow, and the money power of the country will endeavor to prolong its reign by working upon the prejudices of the people until wealth is aggregated in a few hands and the Republic is destroyed. I feel at this moment more anxiety for the safety of my country than ever before, even in the midst of the war." - President Abraham Lincoln

If that's not enough to convince the American patriot, perhaps we should consider more warnings by former U.S. Presidents.

"Whoever (the Federal Reserve System) controls the volume of money in any country is absolute master of all industry and commerce." - President James Garfield.

"History records that the money changers (the Federal Reserve System) have used every form of abuse, intrigue, deceit, and violent means possible to maintain their control over governments by controlling money and its issuance. - President James Madison

"You are a den of vipers and thieves and I intend to rout you out; and by the eternal God, I will rout you out. If Congress has the right to issue paper money, it was given to

them to be used by themselves, and not to be delegated to
individuals or corporations."- President Andrew Jackson

"The Federal Reserve is answerable to no one." - President
Ronald Reagan

Obviously, President Ronald Reagan's statement on the
Federal Reserve System contradicts what the Federal
Reserve System actually state on its official website;
www.federalreserve.gov which states that:

"The Federal Reserve is accountable to the public and the
U.S. Congress." - Federal Reserve System

So, was President Ronald Reagan wrong or lying? Are
former Presidents who have dealt with the tyranny and
corruption from central banks also mistaken or lying? Are
central banks honest and decent hard-working entities who
really care for the economy of its serving nation? The
answer is obvious according to one more final reference
from the actual U.S. President himself (Woodrow Wilson)
who signed the Federal Reserve Act into law, thus
establishing the United States of America with a third
central bank destined to free the economy, but secretly
designed to enslave the economy.

*"I am a most unhappy man, I have unwittingly ruined my
country. A great industrial nation is controlled by its
system of credit. Our system of credit is concentrated. The*

growth of the nation, therefore, and all our activities are in the hands of a few men. We have come to be one of the worst ruled, one of the most completely controlled and dominated governments in the civilized world; no longer a Government by free opinion, no longer a Government by conviction and the vote of the majority, but a Government by the opinion and duress of a small group of dominant men." - President Woodrow Wilson

It is essential and necessary to mention the devaluation of the Federal Reserve Notes, since its initial establishment in 1913, all the way up into 2016 to see for yourself and with your very own eyes, how much our currency which we use to pay our rent/mortgage with, purchase groceries, and send our children to school, has devalued; thus ensuring the Federal Reserve's ultimate purpose: To ensure that the majority of Americans, overtime, work more for less; instead of working less for more which is what can be established with an interest-free currency; thus stabilizing the United States economy and giving the power back to Congress to control all monetary policies instead of a ruthless corporation whose only sole purpose as a banking institution is to enhance their profits by stealing from the American people, thus burdening and enslaving them with infinite debt that can never be repaid back. One dollar in 1913, (the same year as the establishment of the Federal Reserve System) was valued at $24.05; and now in 2016, one dollar is only worth $1.00. That's right; one dollar *since 1913, has devalued by 2,305.4%. If that's not evil, cruel, inhumane, and an irresponsible monetary solution, then we are headed off the cliff to our own graves which are already dug for us, and by us; while the evil and ruthless bankers pointed and laughed at our ignorance and naivete. No longer will this occur as we unite to revolt against the bankers. How much was $100.00, in 1913, compared to 2016 today, after all that time of our beloved currency devaluing, $100.00 is currently worth $100.00 today. But in 1913, $100.00 was worth $2,405.37. The devaluation percentage is 2305.4%. Is this not another system of slavery? As a result of the Federal Reserve Notes devaluing over time, the result was inevitable. Americans will have to work longer and more hours of work, just to make ends meet. And it's only getting worse. It will continue to get worse unless the Federal Reserve System is destroyed and replaced with something more beneficial to the people and everlasting; in terms of being beneficial and prosperous. It is the noble, ethical, and moral thing to do; to liberate and save mankind from debt and ruthless & unnecessary tyranny at the hands of a few dominant bankers whose sole purpose is to destroy the U.S economy; regardless if current politicians disagree with this conclusion. The reality is here and it is happening. It is time for proper legislation to be submitted to Congress and passed by Congress, and signed into law by the current President to ensure safe and tranquility monetary policies.*

Americans deserve this, need this, appreciate this, and must embrace this to live to see the existence of the United States of America as an independent nation.

-Requiring all students to be educated by instructors in all high schools, public or private, on establishing and stabilizing credit in their lives and the rewards and consequences of stabilizing credit and ruining credit-

It's no secret that credit is destroying this great country that we live in. Many bankruptcy's have been declared and established by people and businesses and even city and state governments, and even quite possibly in the future, the federal government because of this "system of credit" that operates within our country. It's quite easy to assume that if a person is qualified with an easy access to a credit line, based on no prior credit history, after applying for credit and getting approved, that the credit-line which is granted to the consumer, is free money to spend with absolutely no consequences. On the contrary, it's the exact opposite! Loans are granted and given with interest, fees, and more hidden fees that are not usually identified to steal money from the consumer. It's a fact; and if credit-card companies and banking institutions deny this or reject this accusation, they're only refusing to admit their involved guilt which is more than somewhat responsible for the recession that happened in our great nation in 2007. Loans were given to consumers who couldn't pay back the loans given to them;

therefore, debt increased for consumers and credit scores
were ruined for millions of Americans as a result of
millions of Americans unable to pay back their loans
and/or mortgages. Today, young adults, usually beginning
at the ages of 18-22, become fascinated with the idea of
being a responsible adult; and this includes getting a
checking-account at a bank and a credit card. The only
problem is, is that young adults are not properly educated
on how to apply for a credit card yet alone even stabilize
their credit report and/or history. Most young adults
believe that if they "pay off a minimum balance on their
credit card statement (their bill), they are responsible
because they are paying off their credit card. But what they
don't realize is they're also ruining their credit score and
adding sums of interest to their payment, and in many cases,
a monthly-minimum-required payment doesn't necessarily
remove the young adult from his or her debt. It only
enhances more debt for the young adult; subconsciously
convincing the young adult that debt is normal and natural;
as it is portrayed in the media in the 21st century when
compared to the 20th and even the 19th century which
literally was non-existent or probably even heard of; with
the exception of applicable city, state, and/or federal taxes.
But on the contrary, debt and deficits are not normal and
are the #1 cause for depression, anxiety, and stress to
Americans in our great nation. If the federal government
wanted to alleviate millions of Americans from these three

*unfortunate feelings and circumstances, (which can be
done by the way with patriotic and noble effort on their
behalf), then why not do so? It is the duty and obligation
for an elected official to make lives easier and convenient
for Americans rather than make it more difficult and
complicated or at least allow ruthless banking institutions
and corporations to make it more difficult and complicated
for Americans. If the government will permit and tolerate
banking institutions and corporations to burden American
society with unnecessary debt, knowing full well that these
entities are causing it, and they are afraid to intervene
through fear of being removed from political force by votes
or by force (assassination), then we do not live in a
Democracy and a safe society. Fear is contagious; and
must be countered at all times when and if it is necessary to
do so. As President Franklin Delano Roosevelt once said:*

*"There is nothing to fear, but fear itself." - President
Franklin Delano Roosevelt*

*But, currently, however, we do have a lot to fear. Many
young-adults, and even older adults, are not being properly
educated about how to build and stabilize credit. Some
people think that this should lie within the parents
jurisdiction and responsibility. The problem is that most
parents in the United States are in the early to mid 20's
range, and they themselves, are not properly educated on
maintaining and stabilizing credit for themselves. Not all*

23

parents, but I would say a great majority of them. Most Americans do not even know that to have adequate credit history is to never surpass your credit-card limit by 30%. For example, if you have a credit line of $200.00, and you spend $59.00 in one or several transactions, then that would leave you around the 29-30% range of spending your limit. If you spend anything more than 30% of your credit card limit, then the three major credit bureaus, (Equifax, Experian, and Transunion) will be glad to report your credit-score as irresponsible and inadequate; thus possibly increasing the consumers interest rates; and impairing them from possibly getting another loan or credit-card in the future. The problem with our current "credit system" is that it's designed to burden the average American consumer with debt. In this case, the federal government has to alternative but to step in and fix this disaster. The only way that this can be repaired is to require all education facilities to begin teaching/instructing all students how to adapt into a credit environment, and to educate them on the rewards of stabilizing credit, and the consequences for not being able to or even attempting to make a payment on your credit-card, loan, etc. As for the instructors/teachers who are educating students on this matter, it should never be a requirement for an instructor/teacher to have sufficient credit on his or her record, in order to qualify as an instructor/teacher to educate students on this matter. Additionally, students must

*be educated for two years in both their junior and senior
year on establishing and stabilizing credit. This bill, which
will be introduced to Congress, will ensure the decrease of
students going into debt in America. These required
courses which should be titled: (unless Congress can think
of a more suitable name) "Credit I,II,III,IV." There should
be two courses a year (I & II for the junior year & III & IV
for the senior year) that are required for all students to
pass in order to successfully graduate from their
designated high school and to receive their high school
diploma. The purpose of this bill, which is supported by the
Enlightened Party is to alleviate and remove unnecessary
potential debt from students who will have likely have
suffered, without the proper education of understanding
how credit operates. It is unfair to many young adults who
enter the ruthless & tyrannical credit environment who are
absolutely uneducated about the dangers of what credit can
bring to an individual; therefore, since major corporations,
are expanding all over America, from grocery stores to
various retail stores who now offer credit cards, it has
become a normal thing in society (its actually more evil
than normal) for everyone to receive a credit and increase
their credit score; but the majority of Americans do not
increase their credit score, on the contrary, they decrease it;
and this is unacceptable. This is cruel and inhumane to
allow the federal government for this to happen.
Government intervention is required and needed to prevent*

any more students from avalanching from a mountain into a landfill of debt. The Enlightened Party believes that the pure distraction of paying off debt, distracts bright, gifted, intelligent, and articulate Americans from achieving success in the future; and those forms of successes can be properly used and manifested into either creating jobs for more Americans, by opening new businesses, expanding businesses, discoveries, and/or inventions. The mind can only bare so much stress and anxiety; and debt is the ultimate cause for this. There will no longer be a question on what is going to be done about this growing threat and concern in America. Corporations are increasing their profits and revenue by burdening American consumers with debt, and the more uneducated and ignorant the American is about credit, will only increase the revenue and profits for these corporations. This must be addressed swiftly; and if the federal government will not intervene on this matter, then the Enlightened Party will intervene for them. That is a promise not a threat!

-A Congressional Bill to require all students in their junior and senior year in high school to be educated on how to open up a new business or establishment in the United States-

It's no secret or lie that the United States has been exporting jobs overseas to countries like China & Vietnam; for the benefit of lower taxes and low-pay-wages for labor in order to export these goods back to America. There are two major problems in America with this result. The first problem is that jobs are becoming more scarce for Americans, and thus the chances of getting a full-time job is becoming more competitive and complicated than it should be. The second problem is since jobs are being transferred to other countries, this means that entrepreneurs are decreasing in America, and not as much of them who keep their jobs in America are being replaced. This means that there are too little entrepreneurs opening businesses in America, and too many Americans looking for work. This means that the demand for employment is high, but the supply is decreasing every day. The good news is that there is a powerful alternative to this crisis; and a beneficial one in the long-run that will literally make the United States superior in job growth; thus employing millions and millions of Americans while ensuring the stability of the U.S. economy. The Enlightened Party proposes to introduce a bill to Congress, requiring all students, in all high schools, public or private, in their respective junior and senior year on how to open up a new business and how to stabilize it. This bill will not require teachers/instructors to have experience on establishing or opening a new business. This bill will require all students in high school to be educated and properly instructed on how to open up a business, expand a business, take over an existing business etc. In order for students to graduate from their designated high schools, student must pass the following courses: (unless Congress designates a more appropriate name for the courses) Entrepreneur Education I,II,III, & IV. Entrepreneurship Education I & II will be required to take in the respected students junior year, while III & IV will be required to take in the respected students senior year. The purpose of this measure and act is to ensure that all Americans who graduate from high school know and understand on how to open a new business, expand a business, or take over a business, which will inevitably result in more entrepreneurs opening new business in America; thus creating hundred of thousands, and perhaps millions and millions of jobs in America; because every future American will now know the complex and appropriate measures on how to open a business based on that persons innovations and creative ideas. I believe that many Americans today, who do not know how to open up a new business or take over an existing business, but who desire it with such great passion, yet never get the chance to do so because these bright and articulate Americans do not know the required steps on how to do so. This discourages many potential entrepreneurs from doing what they are capable of doing best: opening a new business or taking over an existing business. However, if future entrepreneurs, fresh out of high school, and entering the adult world, knew how to open up a business or take over a business, then more jobs would be created and produced. The unemployment rate would drop significantly. The demand for employment would be lower (than what it is today), and the supply would be high (when compared to its low-supply today). All it takes one brilliant mind to grant employment to a handful of Americans, to a hundred employees, to a thousand employees, and even tens of thousands of employees, there are no limits. However, the problem is that this has not happened yet. I say yet because it will happen as The Enlightened Party will ensure that this bill reaches Congress and receives the 2/3rds majority vote, in addition the signature from the current or future U.S President. Anyone who opposes this measure will either subconsciously support the high unemployment rate (about 15-20% today) that our great nation faces today or consciously supports the current high-unemployment rate through fear of competition that may destroy current businesses because of inevitable entrepreneurs who will establish similar businesses in the market. Regardless, of this bills support or opposition, it is the right and noble thing to do to require all 50 states in America to require students to learn the business industry, just in case, a future entrepreneur can open a new business, and create more jobs for Americans. The results will be unanimous if this bill is considered and passed. Unemployment will decrease, as it should be, and as a result of more jobs being established, less competition to obtain a job will likewise decrease, and as a result of millions of Americans obtaining employment, more Americans will be inclined to spend and purchase goods which would inevitably generate revenue for the U.S. economy. This would ensure prosperity for our nation in terms of adequate economic policies and make the U.S. economy stabilized. If the federal government will not intervene on this matter, The Enlightened Party will ensure that this bill has a fighting chance to be passed in Congress, as there is every absolute benefit to every United States citizen that this bill passes and is signed into law.

-Term Limits for All U.S. Presidents, Congressman, Senators, and Supreme Court Justices-

Currently, there are two terms (of four years) for current U.S. Presidents that add to a total of eight years for the possibility of a U.S. President to be reelected once again for another term of four years. However, The Enlightened Party does not support this generous opportunity for the U.S. president to be reelected. A U.S. President should only have one opportunity, one chance, and one term of four years to demonstrate to the American people that he or she is able and capable of protecting our great nation, stabilizing our economy, and ensuring that unemployment is its lowest rate, or non-existent. Other factors matter as well. The U.S President, whether it be a him or her, should only have one opportunity to make his or her name in history as either a great, neutral, or terrible President. This is fair, and this law or statute should apply to the Vice

President, if he or she ever has to take over the duties of the
office of the President of the United States, due to the
President being impeached, resigning, arrested (through
charges), and/or experiencing death in office; and if the
Vice President takes over a term, regardless, if the
finishing term has one, two, three, or almost four years left
to within its term, the Vice President cannot run as
President for reelection. However, the Vice President can
run for President if the Office of the President of the United
States is temporarily given to the Vice President for no
more than sixty days while the President is unable to
execute the office of the President of the United States due
to an injury as such examples.

Congressman/Congresswoman currently have election
terms of two years; and have no limits in regards to being
reelected. This needs to change! I propose, at the maximum
rate of election cycles, three two-year terms for a maximum
of six years as a Congressman/Congresswoman. This will
ensure the very same idea that every
Congressman/Congresswoman who gets elected into office
has two-six years to make their name in history has a
politician who either provided great, neutral, or negative
service to the American people. Too many career-
politicians get reelected but do little or nothing to bring
positive-transitioning policies or bills to the American
people that benefit the majority of Americans. This needs to
change; all future Congressman/Congresswoman will no

*longer have the opportunity to remain in office for decades;
despite the fact that some Congressman/Congresswoman
have left a positive legacy for themselves and have helped
nurture the U.S. economy among other crucial policies that
still require care and rehabilitation.*

*Currently, U.S. Senators serve a term of a minimum of six
years, with every possibility of being reelected for another
six years, for unlimited reelection cycles. This has to stop!
Every state in America has two senators, with a total of 100
senators representing their designated state, but many
senators, remain as senator, by getting reelected, time and
time again, without leaving something positive for the
American people. Most senators in today's society, get
elected, and forget or choose to forget what they promised
to do to the American people during their campaign.
Promises are made; and destined to be broken. Its a fact;
and the result is mistrust and disappointment from the
American people to the politicians who are supposed to be
representing them; but instead begin to represent their own
interests. I often ask myself, which politician would not be
proud to make his or name in history by changing America
for the better, not just for our generation, or the previous
existing generations, but for future generations (our
posterity)? I believe without any doubt or hesitation, that
the majority of politicians who run a successful campaign,
and successfully get elected (or reelected), have positive
intention upon entering office, but for one or several*

*reasons alone, these same politicians who just got elected
or reelected, do not follow on their promises, as if they're
afraid to act on their promise. Their political promises
were not fiction; they were innovations that the American
people determined can be completed and done, and that is
why the voters cast their ballot for that politician who
promised them "capable & adequate policies" but did not
act upon them. I'm not saying that all elected politicians
who were once in office, or are currently in office, are liars
and deceivers. Some are, some aren't. One thing is clearly
obvious, as the majority (if not all) of Americans know and
understand, that politicians will say or do anything in the
pre-election process just to get enough votes to get elected.
It's pathetic, a waste of time, and makes the election-
process a joke. What politicians have done, and are
currently doing, are breaking people's trust which is never
okay. It is wrong and makes a bad name for the politicians
who actually care for the American people and actually
want to do good for the people, and for the society, and for
the country. Nonetheless, senators should only be given two
opportunities to make their name in history and leave
either a positive, neutral, or negative legacy for their
constituents. This means, that all current and future
senators should only be given at the maximum rate, and
limit, two terms of six years, totaling up to 12 years in
office. Senators would no longer be able to run for
reelection for the third time as they have exceeded the limit*

after the second successful attempt of being reelected. As
for Supreme Court Justices, The Enlightened Party favors
term limits for them as well; with a maximum rate of eight
years in office, and upon entering the ninth year, the
Supreme Court Justices should and will be replaced for
another qualified magistrate that is fit to serve and
represent the people of the United States of America. The
Enlightened Party believes that term limits for
Congressman/Congresswoman, Senators, Presidents, and
Supreme Court Justices should be carefully considered and
proposed to Congress, without biased opinions, (which will
inevitably occur) and successfully passed into law, and
signed into law by the current or future U.S. President.
This will guarantee that corrupt politicians who inevitably
enter the chambers of Congress, upon being elected, will
eventually be replaced with another member of Congress,
or Supreme Court Justice, or U.S. President. Regardless, if
a politician demonstrates great moral and positive
performance while in office, and actually offers positive
significant change, in terms of proposing bills that benefit
the majority of the American people, the risk of allowing
any member of Congress, or a Supreme Court Justice, or a
U.S. President, to be reelected without any limits is a
national security threat both to the American people and to
the United States. It is time for the American people to
consider the idea that their federal politicians who
represent them, are capable of being corrupt and paid for

*by corporations in order to suit (the corporations) their
needs and agenda. It is also time for the American people
to begin considering this proposal to permanently establish
term limits for all members of Congress, Supreme Court
Justices, and all current and future U.S. Presidents. There
is every single benefit to do so, and every single loss, not to
do so. What will you do?*

- Abolish the Electoral College-

*How does the corrupt system of the Electoral College work,
you might ask? You might also ask why do we even need it,
if the American people cast their votes for U.S. President,
yet don't really decide the Presidency as delegates decide
the outcome of the Presidential election? Well, first of all,
the Electoral College, was (and still is) a compromise
between the Congress and the American citizens who cast
their ballots. The founding fathers didn't want to give
Congress the absolute power to oversee the presidential
election process, and were too concerned to allow citizens
to select the President and elect him by popular vote, so the
idea proposed, which sadly exists today, is that voters, on
the first Tuesday, on election day, cast their vote for
President, but in reality their casting their votes for the
delegate who will then cast their vote for that President
(the majority of the time, but not always). There are
literally 538 electors (535 from the total number of House
of Representatives and Senators in Congress, and 3 from*

Washington D.C.) who decide the outcome of the Presidency; voters elect the delegates who will more than likely cast their vote for that President, if the President wins the popular vote for that State. Most of the time, this happens, but there have been exceptions, where this will not happen. The point of the matter is, is that we rely on 538 people to decide the fate and outcome of the Presidential election, trusting these people with good faith, that they will keep their word and vote for the President that we, the people, have cast our vote for. Some don't! That is one problem. Another problem is that 538 delegates, a very small proportionate of our entire population compared to over 400 million American citizens should not be deciding the presidential election. Only the voters, votes should go towards the presidential elections, and not a chosen delegate to cast their vote at their designated state convention, upon being selected as a delegate from their political party affiliation. Why do votes from American votes only count towards municipal, state and even congressional elections (House of Representatives & Senators) who represent our city, state, and federal government, but we actually need delegates to decide the outcome of the Presidency? This is absurd; and some people may even forget the very possibility of an opportunity of delegates being bought off from powerful bankers and corporations to vote for a specific presidential candidate that will benefit their (the bankers and

*corporations) agenda, at the expense of many American
citizens, or to change their vote from one designated
candidate to another candidate upon the request from
powerful bankers and corporations. This is not a
conspiracy theory; for if it was, why do Americans mistrust
their government more than ever today, than in the history
of our country? There's a reason for that! There's a reason
for everything. Current politicians have broken the trust
from their constituents and as a result, millions of
Americans refuse to vote, either for one (or several) of six
reasons:*

1. *Their votes don't count!*
2. *Politicians are corrupt and will not follow through
   on their pledged promises!*
3. *Politics don't interest a particular American!*
4. *While politics may interest a particular American,
   there is clearly no time for that interested American
   to read the history and proposals of one or all of the
   candidates that may interest that particular
   American.*
5. *The Voter may be a felon; thus, he or she is
   disqualified from casting their votes for elections.*
6. *The voter will not like any of the participating
   candidates running for office; as they have no
   impressive or interesting personality or history on*

*their background, or any proposed ideas that are
not interesting, intriguing, or controversial enough
to make absolutely powerful & positive changes for
the majority of Americans that will benefit them and
their posterity in the future.*

*If, you're reading this manifesto, what is the reason, why
you quit voting, or if you don't vote? As I mentioned earlier,
there is a reason for everything. People don't do things for
no reason, people do things for a very beneficial reason,
whether it be good or bad choices for themselves or for the
world. What this country needs is an election process for
the presidential elections to be chosen of the people, for the
people, and by the people. While delegates may be people,
538 people are people that are really given supernatural
power & authority to make a decision that can affect our
very great nation that we reside in. The majority of the
American population, should be the ones to determine the
outcome of the Presidential election, since the majority of
Americans who vote in Presidential elections, are tens of
thousands of millions of Americans compared to 538
"alleged-qualified-electors" who are no better or superior
than the average American who participates in elections,
whether it be every election, every other election, or every
so often. The United States of America is a nation that
symbolizes and represents, and is supposed to at all times,*

*the concepts and principles of "equality" & "liberty." The
Electoral College does not symbolize or represent either of
these definitions. A delegate is a delegate because a
political party affiliation, and convention has determined
the qualifications of a "specific" delegate to see to it that
the political party's wanted and chosen presidential
candidate is elected. Certainly, a political party convention
will not give this responsibility to the average American
voter. An American voter must first demonstrate a
consistent affection of loyalty to their political party and
have an impeccable history and record of volunteering
their services or actually working with an elected official
while he or she is in office, who is of the same political
party affiliation, in order to qualify as a respected delegate.
This is not equality! This is pure favoritism and contradicts
American values and principles. There are far more
qualified American voters who deserve to be delegates,
who may not have had a fortunate opportunity to work with
an elected official while he or she was in office, or is
currently in office or contributed towards offering any
volunteer services and/or campaign contributions towards
candidates of their political party affiliation, or donations
(due to unforeseen circumstances and/or events), yet these
loyal voters who have consistently voted for candidates of
their identical political party affiliation, time and time
again, without switching political parties or who never
missed voting during an election, are unfit and not*

*qualified to be a delegate. This is also absurd and makes no
sense. For this reason, The Enlightened Party proposes
that the Electoral College be abolished, and instead of
delegates selecting the President in every Presidential
election, the average and common American voter will
decide the outcome and the election for the President of the
United States of America by popular vote based on the
highest amount of votes that are given to the presidential
candidate. No longer, will 538 American citizens select &
choose the President who will administer economic,
national-security, & controversial policies during his or
her administration; rather, the tens of millions of
Americans will decide the fate and future of America by
casting their votes for the candidate that they see fit and
qualified to represent them as commander-in-chief (in
charge of all military branches) and their President (who is
literally in charge of almost all economic policies despite
what Congress or others believe otherwise). Abolishing the
Electoral College, will begin a positive transition for the
United States of America to allow all future Presidents to
be elected by popular vote, by the tens of millions of
Americans, to decide the fate and outcome in American
history, by electing the most qualified and capable
President of their choosing. This is fair and equal towards
all qualified citizens who intend, decide, or are capable of
voting in all current & future presidential elections. If the
federal government will not exterminate and obsolete this*

election process (the Electoral College), then it is the duty and obligation of The Enlightened Party to intervene in Congress, and successfully abolish the Electoral College and leave the outcome and fate of the Presidential election to the majority of the American people. To intervene in this matter is patriotic, and not to interfere, it's cowardly and letting the American people down. The Enlightened Party cannot allow this to happen as if we continue to allow this to happen and occur, more faith and trust in the government, for all the right reasons will continue to remain broken; and the only way to fix something that is broken is to permanently replace something that is gone, lost, destroyed, or no longer works. The Electoral College no longer works for the benefit of the country and the majority of the citizens who reside in it. Therefore, it's only a matter of time that it's replaced of its power to the 538 delegates, and that power is given to the people of this great country. This is no threat; its a promise. The Electoral must and will be destroyed.

-Tuition-free College-

Tuition-free college is not a new idea, and The Enlightened Party cannot receive credit for creating its idea, but it sure as hell can receive credit for making its cause happen or establishing it for the benefit of each and every American, while an elected politician in Congress; while authoring the appropriate bill and submitting it to Congress for the

purpose of passing it into law and upon being voted on and
passed through Congress, and signed into law by the
current U.S. President. Currently, and never-before in
American history, has college-tuition ever been so
expensive. College-tuition, whether it be a community
college or a university, seem to increase their tuition prices,
for the purposes of either profits or paying increasing-tax-
rates to the state and/or federal governments which always
increases, and never decreases. The price that has to be
paid is that current-college students have to pay high
tuition-rates just to get a decent education when compared
to their parents or their grandparents who paid
significantly lower tuition-rates than their posterity; and
benefited with a better economy, and less competition for
jobs, because of the lower population (respectfully) and
significant low-interest rates that didn't effect their much
then-valuable currency when compared to today, which has
devalued significantly. The Enlightened Party, and its
members, and followers, recognize the important of a great
education to a human-being and what it can offer to that
human-being, and his or her service, based on the
education that he or she has received, can offer to his or
her fellow people and to the world. Americans who seek
higher-intelligence and a great education and is rejected
from doing so because of either high-competition to get
into a great school or because of sky-rocketing tuition-rates
does not and never will represent the American values and

*symbolization of liberty for which America stands for. To
only say, that the upper-middle class, or higher-class
students who can afford to get a decent education (based
on their parents salary) is ridiculous and pathetic. It
contradicts true American values; and prevents our nation
from progressing and elevating as dying-superior nation
when it comes to education. First of all, before I discuss
how much revenue will be needed and/or required in order
to cover the costs of all tuition-free colleges and
universities, and which New Department (which should &
will replace the Department of Education) will oversee this
these policies take affect, and exactly how this will be paid
for and done, (which it can be done despite some
politicians accusations of its impossibility) we must discuss
the reason for this proposal, as there is a reason to change
the current corrupt system of skyrocketing tuition-rates and
student loan debt. So, who benefits from students going into
debt as those very same American students take out loans
from banks and the Department of Education?*

*The answer: Big banks (Bank of America, Chase, and Wells
Fargo) which are too big to fail, (despite what politicians
say that they're not) and the federal government (The
Department of Education).*

*How much do American students owe the ruthless bankers
and the corrupt U.S. Federal Government?*

*The Enlightened
Party Manifesto
(Its Principles &
Ideologies)*

*Currently, American students owe over a trillion dollars of
student-loan-debt to both the ruthless banks and the
corrupt federal government combined. When just looking at
the student-loans given to American students from the
Department of Education, its is well over 400 billion
dollars, in fact, It is estimated by their very own department,
that within a few years (from today's year of 2016), the
Department of Education will exceed over a trillion dollars
of loans to American students. A trillion dollars of student
loans in addition to interest, in which American students
will have to somehow figure out how to pay off their
balance before defaulting, as most students in today's
struggling economy will sadly inevitably do because in
order to pay off such a high-existing balance, (which only
increases over time because of the interest for each loan) is
to obtain an occupation that will pay decent enough in
order to pay the student-loan balance off, and the only
problem with this expectation, is that this expectation is
becoming rare in todays high-unemployment rate, or if
there is employment available, often, the wages are not
enough to make ends-meet; (pay your rent, purchase
groceries, health/car insurance, additional necessities if
you have any children, etc.) and if these people are
struggling to pay their rent (the Average American student)
in addition to crucial necessities that they need and require,
how are these American students going to pay off their
student-loan debt when their student-loan debt is in the tens*

44

*of thousands of dollars? Also, what are the consequences
for not paying off your student-loan debt?*

**Your credit will be destroyed!!! It will be very difficult for
you to obtain an apartment, get certain occupations that
require an adequate credit score (the armed forces &
some corporations), obtain a vehicle through credit at a
dealership, or even get a loan for a new home that is every
American's dream to own someday!**

*Credit & loans are evil. They are designed for one ultimate
purpose; and that is to enslave & burden the borrower with
more debt, until he or she cannot pay anything back, and
will rack up additional charges, interest, and fees. The
more the borrower owes, the more profits skyrocket for any
creditor, banking institution, or lending institution who
distributes the loan to the borrower. The Enlightened Party,
and its members and followers, will always support any
proposed law or statute that will officially destroy the
practice of credit in our great country, or at least remove
the practice of any loan to be issued without any interest;
although, as a competitive business, I would completely
understand any business, in order to generate profit, to
sustain their business, to establish any charges or fees
necessary to sustain their business, except interest that
obviously lasts for decades even a person's lifetime (in
many cases) which is what creditors, banking-institutions,
and other applicable lending-institutions openly (its not a*

secret anymore) want for each and every American. Now,
is the time for tuition-free college, and the most important
& powerful reasons on why our great nation must initiate
& implement this generous and compassionate opportunity
all Americans are the following:

1. *Currently, Germany, Spain, and Italy offer tuition-*
    free college to all of their citizens. These countries
    are nowhere as near as powerful or economically
    powerful as the United States of America, even
    when it comes to having a superior military force.
    Yet, these nations have instituted this measure to
    compete against other nations, so the desire for
    higher-education will pose no obstacles & barriers
    towards that civilian who desires high-education.
    The possibility is there upon request. Why aren't we
    doing the same thing for ourselves and our future
    posterity? What will it take to see this happen? All it
    really takes is courage from an elected-politician in
    Congress to author the measure, and gain the
    majority of support from the American voters, and
    of Congress. We cannot allow other nations to offer
    something better to their civilians, and we do not
    offer the very same thing. We must compete against
    other nations, if we are to remain a superior nation,
    in terms of education & advanced technology which
    is discovered & invented by men and women who
    are experienced (thanks to higher-education) in

*specific fields that enables him or her to be overly-
qualified and confident to make a discovery or an
invention that is credited to yet another American,
which can and will always be a great thing to our
nation. If we deprive Americans access to tuition-
free college, then we deprive ourselves as a nation
to discover and invent more beneficial, essential,
and crucial things and opportunities that can
elevate mankind to superior, powerful, and
prosperous changes that will always come with a
benefit, in which mankind can live more convenient
and easier for the better, and certainly never for the
worse.*

2. *Student-loans, either individually, (from the
Department of Education), or in conjunction with
banks is a system that operates successfully
(unfortunately) to burden and enslave every
American student who desires and seeks higher-
education, with debt that literally lasts several years
to perhaps a few decades. It's no joke! Debt is a
normal and horrible thing in our nation. The
majority of the population (The American student)
suffers as a result of this national tyranny, while a
small population of people (bankers, creditors, &
politicians) benefit off the most. This is a major
problem. Debt is not a normal thing; it was never
intended by the founding fathers of our great nation*

*to burden the majority of Americans with debt in
order to seek and obtain higher-education. This
only became an issue in the late 20th century and it
is certainly an issue in the 21st century. The
situation is getting worse with no possible solutions.
Even if the nation currently has a 0.0 unemployment
rate, and the job market was excellent, and the
economy was superior, it is immoral and wrong to
allow an American to pay off student-loan debt with
tens of thousands of dollars in debt just to get a
decent education, which with it, comes every
opportunity for a discovery or invention to be made
based on learning something in school, which was
previously not known before entering college. The
average American student in the United States, has
debt ranging between $28,000-$33,000 and even
more, and rarely less. Over 40 million Americans
are in student-loan debt. Note: this does not include
any other debt that the average American currently
has, through either personal credit cards, or car-
payments; among other elements of debt which
ultimately leads to more poverty and stress for the
average American. This burden certainly does bring
any relief or pleasure to the average American. **Do
the majority of Americans deserve to be stressed
out and enslaved with unnecessary debt that other**

48

countries refuse to do to their own citizens? The
answer is unequivocally no!!!

3. *The billions of dollars, which will soon turn into*
    trillions of dollars, if there is no government
    intervention to stop this crisis, will be a disaster and
    generate devastating turmoil to our economy, which
    is still struggling to recover. Excessive debt that
    adds to the national debt and the nation's deficit is a
    danger to national security; despite what politicians
    say or think that "it's not!" It is a national security
    threat, because if students default on their student-
    loan debt, the government defaults as well. This is
    a problem that needs to be addressed. We cannot
    allow the corrupt-elite bankers and creditors to
    continue making skyrocket profits at the expense of
    innocent American students. If education comes as
    a price in America, we no longer should perceive
    ourselves as a nation that represents & symbolizes
    liberty, freedom, prosperity, and equality. We must
    avert this threat that exists to make our country
    extinct of its original principles & ideologies that
    was established by our founding fathers.

How are we going to pay for tuition-free college, you may
be wondering or asking yourself? It's simple, there are two
ways to do it! Raise taxes to achieve this Amendment or
Bill, or to cut spending. I propose raising taxes on all of the
largest banks who currently operate within all the

territories of the United States and cutting spending. Here is my plan to tax the very same corrupt banking institutions who were responsible for our recession in 2007, and who still benefit on enslaving the American student with student-loan debt.

1. *21 of the largest banking institutions in the United States, including, but not limited to future operating banks (which are yet to exist which upon existing will be subjected to paying the same amount of tariffs as the other largest banking institutions), Bank of America, Wells Fargo, JPMorgan Chase, Citigroup, Goldman Sachs, Morgan Stanley, U.S. Bankcorp, Bank of New York Mellon, PNC Financial Services, Capital One, HSBC Bank USA, State Street Corporation, TD Bank N.A, BB&T, Suntrust Banks, American Express Company, Ally Financial, M&T Bank, Fifth Third Bank, Citizens Financial Group, & Charles Scwab Corporation, will be required individually, and annually, to pay a three (3) billion-dollar tax to the Department of Education who will then see to it that the funds received by the numerous & various banks are distributed to numerous & various colleges & universities to cover the cost of tuitions and all other applicable fees. Since there is currently 21 large banking institutions in America, 21x3=63 billion-dollars in*

*generated revenue from the banking institutions
that will be given to the Department of Education.
Anything left over as a "surplus," from this
amount will be saved by the Department of
Education as a reserve in any event, any of the
following banking institutions default on their tax
or file for bankruptsy. It is not be spent on
anything other than tuition and fees at all
recognized colleges and universities, whether they
would be private or public.*

2. *I am for cutting spending in departments or
eliminating certain departments completely that
serve no purpose or do not offer sensible and
beneficial circumstances and/or events, or
solutions towards the American people. In this
case, cutting foreign aid by 20 billion dollars
annually, (we currently spend about 35 billion
dollars a year) would be an additional reserve to
increase the surplus of paying for tuition and fees
to all colleges and universities. The 20 billion
dollars that will be deducted from foreign-aid
spending will be reserved only as an emergency to
cover the cost of tuition and fees for all public and
private colleges and universities.*

*For those politicians who are currently in office and
concerned Americans who oppose cutting foreign aid to
other countries, they have every right to their opinion and*

beliefs regarding this matter. It is compassionate & generous that they feel concern for other nations that require American assistance & aid. I also can support this, but I believe that the American people come first and their concerns, securities, and opportunities. Without a decent college education, especially a college education that is guaranteed, regardless of income status, concern of debt is severely reduced. Security for the American people and our economy is apparent, and the infinite opportunities in America are no longer limited or a "fairy-tale" which contradicts our American values & principles. The Enlightened Party does believe in foreign-aid only upon request and a small-generous donation of a couple billions of dollars. If we can spend 35 billion dollars a year on foreign-aid, (half of which will cover the cost to put every American student in college), worrying about other civilians in other nations, than we are clearly on the wrong path. We must first fix and resolves our education and debt crisis before we begin to help & aid other nations, even if those nations who are asking for our assistance, are our very own allies. We must protect and help the American people first, and this will be done, regardless of political opposition. Many critics, including wealthy bankers and politicians will laugh and condemn this proposed idea because The Enlightened Party proposes to tax 21 banking institutions by 3 billion dollars. They (the politicians, lenders, creditors, & bankers), will possibly threaten another economic collapse because it hurts their businesses but it was these banks who helped bankrupt this nation to begin with, them and the infamous Federal Reserve System. ***All of these banks may deny responsibility to the 2007 recession, but they can never deny the fact that they profit off of putting people in debt, particularly American students through student-loans which are packed with fees and interest that takes years, and perhaps a few decades to pay off!*** *The banks do not deserve any rewards or compassion for their abusive practices. They deserve to be taxed just as much as they have illegally done to the American people. They do not deserve mercy, as they have not given mercy to the American people. Therefore, The Enlightened Party has proposed the idea to tax them 3 billion dollars a year to a total of 63 billion dollars to cover the cost of tuition and all fees for all American students at all colleges and universities, whether it be public or private. This is justice and mercy to the American people; and a threat and a promise, to all ruthless banking institutions.*

-Abolishing the Federal Reserve System-

Although, we discussed earlier in the book, the proposal of an interest-free currency, and the abolition of the Federal Reserve System briefly, The Enlightened Party will like to make it further clear into detail on how to abolish the Federal Reserve System. This will require every elected politician who's loyalty is with The Enlightened Party to each author a bill (if they're a Congressman/Woman) abolishing the Federal Reserve System, to make its corrupt system null and void, and to propose an Amendment (if they're a Senator) to make it legal for the United States of America to forbid and make illegal any current and future central bank in the United States of America. The Federal Reserve System, is our third national bank in our great nation, who is responsible for stabilizing the economy, while controlling inflation in regards to the Federal Reserve Notes, which is the very same currency that Americans use every day to purchase necessary essentials. The Federal Reserve does neither of these objectives and priorities that it is supposed to do, and was supposed to do upon it being established. I guess that's the reason why it's our third national bank, because obviously within 44 presidential administration, two central banks (The First Bank of the United States & The Second Bank of the United States) have failed in history due to its abusive practices & policies, and were rejected, opposed, and abolished by previous Presidents (President James Madison & President Andrew Jackson) for its obstruction and enslavement on the American people. These former central banks, and our current Federal Reserve System operated in secret, and still continue to operate in secret, for two purposes:

1. *To dominate the United States into a nation consisting of infinite & everlasting debt.*

2. *To enslave every hard-working American with debt.*
3. *To make the U.S. government dependent on their corrupt system of lending.*
4. *To permanently eliminate the middle-class & establish the rich class to dominate the poor class.*

Let us never forget the words of Federal Reserve Chairman Ben Bernanke:

"Importantly, in the 1930's, in the great depression, the Federal Reserve, despite its mandate, was quite passive, and as a result, financial crisis became very severe, lasted essentially from 1929 to 1933." - Federal Reserve Chairman Ben Bernanke

This former Federal Reserve Chairman recognizes the great responsibility that the Federal Reserve System had on the economy during the great depression. He knew that the Federal Reserve System did everything it could to allow to happen, and did nothing to stop or prevent it. It was the worst economic depression that our country ever faced in the history of our country. The Federal Reserve System failed the American people in the 1920's, and 1930's, and its corrupt system is still failing us in the 21st century, even in the current year, 2016 as this book is being written. There is something very strange about how the Federal Reserve System operates; according to the Federal Reserve

Systems, actual website, www.federalreserve.gov, on their frequently asked questions list, the following is published:

"As the nation's central bank, the Federal Reserve derives its authority from the Congress of the United States. It is considered an independent central bank because its monetary policy decisions do not have to be approved by the President or anyone else in the executive or legislative branches of government, it does not receive funding appropriated by the Congress, and the terms of the members of the Board of Governors span multiple presidential and congressional terms. However, the Federal Reserve is subject to oversight by the Congress, which often reviews the Federal Reserve's activities and can alter its responsibilities by statute. Therefore, the Federal Reserve can be more accurately described as "independent within the government" rather than "independent of government."

This is certainly not accurate; as we all know and recognize the substantiated fact that every single bill that has been proposed to Congress to audit the Federal Reserve System has always received threatening responses from the Federal Reserve, especially from its own former chairman's (Ben Bernanke) and current chairman (Janet Yellen) who are appointed by the U.S. President himself. If The Federal Reserve System claims that it is not "independent of government," then why are is its corrupt

*and tyrannical system so opposed to audits by the federal
government? Isn't the Federal Reserve System supposed to
be "independent within the government," as it claims,
rather than "independent of government?" Apparently, that
has never been the fact, and it is still not a fact, that "the
Federal Reserve is subject to oversight by the Congress,
which often reviews the Federal Reserves activities, and
can alter its responsibilities by statute." An H.R. Bill
(proposed to Congress by Congressman/Congresswoman)
or Amendment (Proposed by U.S. senators) is a proposed
statute to make something lawful, valid, and/or legal, which
either abolish a law, propose regulations to an existing law,
or amend (edit or correct) a law. It's no secret that
Congressman Ron Paul and his son, Senator Rand Paul
have proposed numerous legislations to either audit or
abolish the Federal Reserve System. However, other
politicians have proposed or co-sponsored similar "audit
the fed" bills to Congress to audit the Federal Reserve
System. This proposal primarily comes from the Republican
Party, and the majority of people who do support "auditing
the fed" are Republicans. I am actually surprised that the
Democrats never have supported these audits or
considered teaming up with Republicans to audit the
Federal Reserve System. The majority of supporters who
support the Democratic Party will and probably assume
that Democratic politicians support and defend the middle-
class and people in poverty; and oppose giving tax-breaks*

*to the wealthy, and criticize corporate America for their
alleged greed against the American people. Democratic
politicians currently attack banking-institutions and blame
them for causing the great recession of 2007, and yet have
always had an opportunity to attack and analyze one of the
true culprits of the great recession of 2007, and still refuse
to do so. Democratic politicians may criticize banking-
institutions for their greed & tyrannical practices, but
establish no record of actually regulating these
"condemned & opposed banks," while Republicans, who
are allegedly in favor of Corporate America & the
banking-institutions, somehow attempt to regulate and
question the very same banking-institution who helped in
the process of nearly bankrupting our nation. I thought
Republicans were in favor of the rich, and allowing them to
monopolize America? If that's the true case, why are
Republican leaders proposing legislation to oversee and
question the activities of our central bank? The answer is
obvious! It's because the Republican Party recognizes the
abusive and tyrannical practices of the Federal Reserve
System; while the Democratic Party still refuses to believe
or support this idea, or is too intimidated (by powerful
sources) to question our central bank? Whatever the case
remains, The Enlightened Party does not support any audit
of the Federal Reserve System. That wastes too much time
and taxpayer money from the American people. Instead, the
Enlightened Party supports the abolition of the Federal*

Reserve System and will do anything & everything legal
and moral to abolish this corrupt & tyrannical system once
and for all; and put in place proper legislation through
Congress to forever forbid and make unlawful, and
unconstitutional in the United States of America, a fourth
or any central bank to oversee all of our economic policies.
Let me also demonstrate Federal Reserve Chairman Ben
Bernanke threatening an economic crisis if the Federal
Reserve System were to be audited.

"Congress is not well-suited to make monetary policy
decisions, itself, because of the technical and time-sensitive
nature of those decisions. Moreover, both historical
experience and formal studies, have shown that monetary
policy achieves better results when central bankers are
allowed to focus on the longer-term interests of the
economy, free of short-term political considerations."
- Federal Reserve Chairman Ben Bernanke

"I know from first-hand experience that the FOMC
(Federal Open Market Committee) sets monetary policy
with the best technical information available and without
any consideration of politics or partisanship. I am also
confident that political interventions in monetary policy
decisions would not lead to better results." - Federal
Reserve Chairman Ben Bernanke

*"The Fed should continue to strive to improve its
transparency and accountability, and in particular to
ensure that Congress has all the information it needs to
fulfill its oversight responsibilities. However, this goal is
not best achieved by overturning longstanding practice and
effectively inserting Congress and the GAO into monetary
policy decisions, calling into question the Fed's
independence." - Federal Reserve Chairman Ben Bernanke*

*"'Audit the Fed' is a bill that would politicize monetary
policy and it would bring short-term political pressures to
bear on the Fed." - Federal Reserve Chairman Janet
Yellen*

*"Central bank independence in conducting monetary policy
is considered a best practice for central banks around the
world, I think, establish beyond the shadow of a doubt that
independent central banks perform better." - Federal
Reserve Chairman Janet Yellen*

**First of all, if Janet Yellen was correct that "independent
central banks perform better" independently, without
interference or intervention, then should we the people, as
Americans, acknowledge American history, that we tried
twice to allow central banks to act independently from the
federal government, and it did not work? The answer is yes!
Too much corruption was imminent and apparent. The
United States was under control from a small-elite of**

bankers who involved themselves in monetary & political decisions. The result was and still is the same thing, the central banks lend the U.S. government money with interest which can never be paid back; since there has never been and nor will there ever be an opportunity or possibility for the federal government to pay the Federal Reserve System back of all its loans to our nation and unknown loans to unknown entities and/or corporations. Government intervention has always been and will always be necessary to review central banks "true agenda" because history will always show without any doubt as well, that almost all central banks in history have failed because of their abusive practices and desire to enslave their serving nation with massive debt; which inevitably destroys that nations economy. The United States economy is nearly destroyed with its current national debt of 19 trillion dollars, which no politician in Congress or even the President himself (Barack Obama) has or can come up with a solution to pay or remove all of this debt. The only way to remove all of this debt would be to first buy back the Federal Reserve System, which the U.S. government can purchase back with 500 million dollars, thus purchasing all the U.S. government bonds that the Federal Reserve System has purchased for nothing, (by creating money out of thin air) from the U.S. government. If this were to happen, the U.S. government upon purchasing backs the Treasury Bonds from the Federal Reserve, would never happen to pay back

*the interest for the Treasury Bonds that the Federal
Reserve would no longer own or possess. Additionally, The
Enlightened Party supports the successful passage of
abolishing the Federal Reserve System, and in favor of
replacing its power to issue currency, would be transferred
to the Treasury of the Secretary as it is his or her duty and
obligation as listed in the United States constitution. Let us
never forget, the current system, which is obviously never
taught in schools to ourselves and our children, on how the
tyrannical Federal Reserve System operates! Since the
Federal Reserve System creates money out of thin air, by
purchasing the U.S. Treasury bonds, this inevitably
increases the money-supply, without the increase of goods
and services, which ultimately & inevitably leads to
inflation. In case, the reader is wondering on how much the
average U.S. Treasury bond is sold to the Federal Reserve
System, It is 3 cents out of $99.97, for every hundred
dollars, because of the cost for the Federal Reserve to print
out the money to purchase the U.S. bond. This means that
the Federal Reserve System profits 99.97% by purchasing
the U.S. Treasury Bond, spending only 0.3%, which
increases the owners of the Federal Reserve System profits
by a powerful & significant margin. The U.S. government is
pretty much throwing away their Treasury Bonds for free
as if it was nothing valuable to begin with. This needs to
end, and it must be stopped! As long as the Federal Reserve
System continues to exist and be in charge of all of our*

nation's monetary policies, unemployment will continue to rise, inflation will continue to rise, and eventually & inevitably hyper-inflation will manifest and the American people will be in a worse situation, catastrophically than the American people were during the great depression. We will no doubt have a second great depression if we allow the Federal Reserve System to continue to purchase our treasury bonds, which they did not earn to purchase. The American people will continue to see their taxes raised, their hard-earned wages garnished, (through the Internal Revenue Service) just to pay off all the interest to the Federal Reserve System; which can and will never be paid back. The only solution and option is legally destroy the Federal Reserve System with appropriate legislation (H.R. bills & Amendments) and/or a physical revolution from the American people. The sooner this is done, the American people will see for themselves the glorious & valuable, & prosperous events & circumstances that our great nation will endure and continue to endure for generations & centuries to come.

-Abolishing the Income Tax-

Along with the passage of the Federal Reserve Act in 2013, was also the passage of the Revenue Act of 1913, which is one of the most deceitful tariff acts ever signed into law to legally steal from American people. Most Americans assume and think, that they're their income taxes go

*towards the civil, state and/or federal government. It goes
to no such operating government. Every American who
works and whose check is garnished due to income taxes,
does not go towards construction, research for cancer or
energy, or even paying off the salaries for local police
officers and firefighters, or social security, or Medicaid, or
Medicare. It does not go to pay for freeways or build
elementary schools for children or even hospitals. Every
cent that is garnished from every Americans hard-earned
paycheck goes directly to pay off the interest off the loans
(which can still never be paid back) in which the infamous
& tyrannical Federal Reserve System have lent to the U.S.
government so the government can pay its bills and operate
our nation. The taxes that get taken away from every hard-
working American only benefits the people who own the
Federal Reserve System; which are stockholders and
unknown people who never reveal their true identities.
These invisible people to the government, and to the people,
enjoy massive profit at the expense of the American people,
through taxation to pay off the interest (in which they
created) that the federal government owes to the Federal
Reserve System because of their loans to the U.S.
government. It is sad and ridiculous; but this is happening;
and it is a living nightmare to the American people. There
are four problems that exist within the Internal Revenue
Service which needs to be addressed and responded with
appropriate legislation that abolishes its agency*

permanently; as it is a corrupt agency designed, alongside the Federal Reserve System, to enslave the American people.

1. *The first problem is that the Internal Revenue Service legally steals money from hard-working Americans to pay off unnecessary interest to multiple loans that the U.S. government can still not figure out how to payback. With 19 trillion dollars, it may take more than a century to pay off all of this debt; no exaggeration here. Even worse, its never likely to be paid back; and more debt will increase overtime to enslave our nation unless both the Federal Reserve System and the Internal Revenue Service are both abolished and finally destroyed.*

2. *The second problem is that the average hard-working American who will either get a tax return or not, can easily calculate that all the "income taxes" garnished throughout the year, have accumulated to the equivalency of the average hard-working American working 3-4 months out of the year for free! That's right, and if you don't believe me, pull out your paystub's and compare them to your tax-returns. In some cases, some Americans work 5-6 months out of the year for free; seeing all their hard-earned funds go straight to the ruthless bankers corporation to pay off the interest in which they benefit comfortably thanks to the*

*politicians who allow this, while their in Congress,
and our President while he is currently in office.
These politicians are not stupid, as they know what
is going on; they are just afraid & intimidated to
speak out against these tyrants because they know
that their life may be in danger or their political
career; or both! It's not a conspiracy theory; it's a
fact; and American history has shown this from time
and time again.*

3. *The third problem is the Internal Revenue Service
does kill small-businesses and corporations; and as
a result, kills jobs, and increases the unemployment
rate in the United States. As long as the Internal
Revenue Service can tax any operating business
whether its stabilized or struggling, the potential
threat for that existing business to operate exists.
Many small businesses struggle to survive because
of the Internal Revenue Service. It is no secret, that
any small-business owner will publicly
acknowledge that that he or she can thrive and
survive with unlimited potential if the Internal
Revenue Service did not exist. Many potential
entrepreneurs who are motivated and inspired to
start a business or take over an existing business,
are discouraged from doing so because of intense
fear from the Internal Revenue Service; as well they
should be (scared but not discouraged), since they*

*understand beforehand, that the Internal Revenue
Service operates only for the mere purpose of
stealing hard-earned money for those who attempt
to work and/or start a business or take over an
existing business.*

4. *The fourth problem with the Internal Revenue
Service is that it legally has the power and authority
to take away all property (homes, vehicles, property,
& belongings) from Americans who refuse to pay
their taxes? Does this sound fair? Why should the
hard-working American pay taxes to make a
handful of ruthless bankers more wealthier than
they already are, who do not even assist with
helping or freeing our economy, but rather
enslaving it with debt and destroying our beautiful
nation? Since the Internal Revenue Service works
directly with the Federal Reserve System, by paying
them their not hard-earned money, can we truthfully
acknowledge that what President Thomas Jefferson
said about central banks are true?*

*"If the American people ever allow private banks to
control the issue of their currency, first by inflation, then
by deflation, the banks and corporations that will grow up
around them will deprive the people of all property until
their children wake up homeless on the continent their
Fathers conquered"* - *President Thomas Jefferson*

*Note, the phrase from above quotation "will deprive the
people of all property," well that is what the Internal
Revenue Service System has done since its establishment,
and what currently does every day for those patriotic
Americans who refuse to pay their taxes. Yes, I call them
patriotic because they're obviously not scared or
intimidated to pay off a ruthless entity that gives free money
(from hard-working Americans) to lazy and ruthless
bankers and stockholders, who could care less about our
economy and the average hard-working American. It's time
to abolish the Internal Revenue Service and give the power
that is designed to dominate the American people; it would
be immoral and inhumane not to intervene on behalf of the
American people regarding this tyrannical organization.
The American people deserve to have their hard-working
tax dollars to themselves and not to a small handful of
ruthless tyrants (bankers) who's only desire is to burden the
majority of Americans with debt and wage-garnishes just to
increase their profits. The Enlightened Party supports the
abolishment of the Internal Revenue Service and to replace
it absolutely nothing. The following reasons are clear and
justified:*

1. *Alleviate and destroy any potential threat to burden
   the American citizen with unnecessary debt which
   only established stress, difficulty, and problems to
   the average American. This needs to stop!*

2. *It will prevent the Federal Reserve System from having control over the American citizens earnings; and they will no longer benefit off the back-breaking American consumers profits.*

3. *It will encourage and establish new businesses in America, since entrepreneurs will be more encouraged and motivated to open a business in America, thus creating jobs, because of the fact that there is no fear or threat from the Internal Revenue Service to tax heavily on the newly-established business and the business owner; and of course, the future employees.*

4. *American citizens, especially families who reside in their home, and who are unable to pay their property taxes, or any taxes directly to the Internal Revenue Service, will no longer fear any threat to "wake up homeless," as they see their home taken away from the U.S. government. From this point on, all Americans who own something to their name, will never have fear from the government to have it taken away from their hands, and from their lives. No exceptions and no apologies!*

-Requiring all Community Colleges in the United States of America to begin issuing Bachelors Degrees-

The Enlightened Party, and its members are disappointed with the fact, that not only is tuition for colleges

69

skyrocketing like-never-before, in the history of our country, but just as equally unfortunate and ridiculous, is the fact that it's becoming more competitive for graduating students (from high school) or trasnfer students from other universities and other applicable educational institutions, to be accepted into the college of their desire, dream, and choice; yet alone get accepted into any college at all, even though the qualifying student may have an outstanding grade-point-average and academic background to their name, and the student or students family is able to cover the tuition-fees. Even students with high ACT scores (American College Testing) or SAT scores (Scholastic Assessment Tests) are being denied access to great colleges and universities. As the population continues to increase, and graduation rates also increase, and more students seek higher-education, regulations for colleges and universities seem to increase, and as a result, it is more difficult for students to be accepted into any college and university, despite their impeccable record of good standing and great leadership skills. There is a great solution to this crisis that plagues and prevents Americans from getting the best opportunity for an education that they so rightfully deserve, yet are challenged and prevented constantly (unlike previous generations) from obtaining higher-education.

There needs to be a federal law that requires all community colleges in the United States of America to begin issuing bachelors degrees to qualifying students, with the same

current regulations and admission requirements that are
for students who apply for admission to their selected
community colleges for an associates degree. There should
be no higher-requirements for a student to receive a
bachelor's degree by paying higher tuition than that student
would normally be paying for an associates degree at their
selected community college.

**Note: Although, the Enlightened Party has disclosed
endorsement and a plan to pay for tuition-free colleges
and universities, the above idea is only if "tuition-free
college" is not yet established as a federal law before
community colleges begin issuing bachelor's degrees at
their designated location.**

*Currently, in most universities and colleges, (with the
exception of Ivy League schools) the following
requirements in order to receive access to that college or
university are the following:*

1. *3.0 Grade-Point-Average*
2. *Excel highly in the SAT Test and/or the Act Test*
3. *Receive two or three letters of recommendations
   from former professors at the students previous
   education institution.*
4. *Have some experience in doing voluntary work
   and/or community service.*
5. *A crime-free record.*

6. *An interview with a representative from the college
    or university that the student applied for admission
    for the coming semester-term.*

*Note: these are just the average and common requirements
for students who are seeking higher-education in their
home state. For out-of-state students, the above
requirements are much more complicated and have higher
regulations. For example, some universities and colleges
will want an out-of-state college student to pay higher
tuition-rates, and have a higher-grade-point average (3.4)
just to be considered for admissions.*

*Most of the requirements needs some severe amending! The
Enlightened Party, and its founder, support the newly-
established idea of every community college in the United
States of America to begin issuing bachelors degrees with
lower regulations than what current colleges and
universities require and request from potential candidates
today. First, community colleges require all their students,
for the most part, to obtain and maintain a 2.0. grade-
point-average prior to graduation and receiving an
associates degree. That needs to remain current with
college students majoring in a specific field in order to
receive an associates degree of their choice. However, I
propose that a new federal law be established to require all
current and future students from either high school or
transferring college institutions to have at the time of*

*admissions at their designated community college, a 2.0.
Grade-Point-Average, and prior to graduating and
receiving his or her bachelor's degree, the student must
have had a current 2.5 grade-point-average. So, again,
here are my proposed requirements for all community
colleges who will begin issuing bachelor's degrees. This
does not apply to other universities and/or other four-year
colleges (at least not yet).*

1. *Upon entering the community college, the student
   must have a minimum of a 2.0 grade-point-average
   in order to get accepted as a student majoring in a
   field in order to receive a bachelor's degree. This
   applies also to out-of-state students.*
2. *Upon graduating from college, and receiving a
   bachelor's degree from the community college of
   their choice, the student must have a minimum of a
   2.5. grade-point-average.*
3. *No interviews should be required by federal law, to
   determine the eligibility of the student.*
4. *No letters of recommendation from former
   professors should be required or requested from the
   community college in order for the applying student
   to be considered for admission at that community
   college.*
5. *No community-service or voluntary work should be
   required or requested from the community college*

in order for the applying student to be considered for admissions at that community college.

6. *As for the crime-free record, with the exception of previous convictions such as rape, robbery, murder, burglary, child-molestation, robbery, extortion, kidnapping, and/or severe felonies (but not all felonies), students who have a history with the law, should be accepted into their designated community college. This is only supported by the Enlightened Party on the basis of "court orders" from courts that require convicted civilians to return to school to receive further education in an effort to rehabilitate their lives by being a law-abiding-citizen.*

Whether the government admits this or not, this is a national security issue that needs to be resolved and fixed immediately. Too many students are qualified to enter into a university and/or four-year college, and are being rejected because there are too many applicants and too many regulations. If Community Colleges, begin issuing bachelor degrees at their locations, more students will be able to live the American dream of earning and receiving a bachelor's degree of his or her choice. A lot more applicants would be approved of receiving higher-education, and a lot less would be rejected from seeking

*higher-education. Overcrowding in the classroom at
various colleges and universities across American would
also decrease significantly. This would put a lot less
pressure on instructors, and in return would provide a
more "stress-free environment." However, national security
would (not could) be jeopardized in America if we continue
the current process of preventing brilliant, articulate,
creative, and intelligent students from achieving higher-
education, the possibility of advancing our great nation
with advanced technology will continue to remain low and
decline. In order for scientists, discoverer's, and/or
inventors to successfully establish their agenda, they must
require the necessary resources that are available to them
(higher education), in order to motivate, inspire, encourage,
and essentially educate them in the process of knowing
crucial information that is necessary in order to make a
discovery and/or invention. For example, there is a theory
that time travel may be possible, according to Stephen
Hawking, when he claimed that:*

*"Time travel used to be thought of as just science fiction,
but Einstein's general theory of relativity allows for the
possibility that we could warp space-time so much that
you could go off in a rocket and return before you set
out." - Stephen Hawking (theoretical physicist &
cosmologist)*

*Whether or not, time travel exists is irrelevant to this point. The point is, is that people who strive to be like Stephen Hawking & Albert Einstein who appreciate and love learning about science and the way our mysterious world operates, is capable of making discovering and/or inventions with the right resources that are available & given to that seeker of advanced knowledge. For example, if a person wanted to build a time machine (realistically), then that person would first have to learn and understand how math and science, and we're talking about advanced science and math, not Algebra I or Biology 101. It will take years and extensive research, and dedication for that eager student who thirsts for knowledge to become an expert in the field of science and math to begin understanding how wormholes work, and how to possibly manipulate them. The resources are available in the United States, (higher education) but resources although, they're unlimited, they're also limited to students because of college-admission-rejections. We're at a wonderful time in history, where the possibilities are unlimited & infinite, to the point, where mankind can really elevate and excel to become even more superior; thanks to current & future articulate, inspiring, creative, & intelligent current college & future students. also do understand that not every inventor and discoverer had a college degree, but what I am attempting to imply, is that **college degrees do and can help in the process!** In order to make the United States of America a* *superior nation above all other nations, we must reconsider the proposal of allowing all community colleges to begin issuing bachelor's degrees to students, who qualify to receive them, and to keep our status as a super-power nation; in terms of advanced technology. The more credit the United States of American can receive & establish by American discoverers & inventors, is the greatest & most valuable asset to our nation. Americans are credited for many great inventions and discoveries ever since it has been founded as a country, beginning with the vehicle, the airplane, the stove, the lightbulb, the discovery of electricity, and the list goes on. What will be our next invention? A time machine? What will be our next discovery? The ability for mankind to manipulate gravity like what possibly happened in the making of the Pyramids of Giza? I'm only speculating the possibilities to unanswered questions. But the point is, is that American students deserve more and deserve better than what they currently have today. We must pass a federal law to require all community colleges in the United States of American to begin issuing bachelor's degrees, with little regulations & requirements, so our nation can continue to excel and surpass every other nation on Earth in education & advanced technology. The Enlightened Party does not request this, it demands this from Congress, and it will be done, with or without opposition from Congress & the President of the United States of America.*

-Returning to the Gold Standard-

*Let's be realistic here; the money that we have in our
wallets and our bank accounts are becoming worthless and
less valuable as each year passes; requiring hard-working
Americans to **"work more for less,"** because inflating the
dollar is beginning to be a normal thing, and somehow it is
tolerated by the American people. Fiat currency that is
printed without anything backed behind it, unless it is
interest-free, is a threat and danger to any nation who
adopts that currency as legal tender. The gold standard in
America has, throughout its history, made the United States
a prosperous and economical nation. Why? Because, the
gold standard brings value to the US dollar. Inflation is
controlled and central banks, if they exist in the nation that
issue currency, are more properly controlled. Food prices
are stabilized; as well as barrels of oil. Without a gold
standard, central banks are authorized by the U.S.
government to print as much money as needed, with or
without accountability (realistically speaking) from the U.S.
government, and as a result of printing money, a secret
hidden tax is established on the American people. That
secret tax is called inflation. Inflation makes our currency
more worthless and less valuable as I have mentioned
previously in this book. There are additional benefits to the
U.S. government once again adopting the gold standard to
back up the currency of the U.S.*

1. *Wages would increase properly for Americans as it always has for Americans who lived during the time when the gold standard was in effect.*
2. *The price of oil would drop, and the price per-gallon at gas stations would also drop.*
3. *Unemployment would shrink as well (literally)*
4. *The gold standard would restrict the U.S. government from printing more money, thus preventing inflation; since the gold standard protects the value of the currency.*

Critics of the gold standard will argue that if the U.S. adopted the gold standard once again to back the U.S. dollar, that if war broke out between the United States and other nations, that the United States of American would not have enough money to pay off the cost of potential wars; as wars are devastatingly expensive and costly. However, the United States has shown from time and time again, that is has been able to deter any danger that threatens the safety of our great nation. The United States won both world wars; while still on the gold standard. In 1971, when President Richard Nixon took us off the gold standard, the United States was at war with Vietnam. Although, the war dragged on for two decades, the United States could have survived economically if President Richard Nixon did not take us off the gold standard like he did. There is a solution to this theory though. If there is not enough gold to back up the U.S. dollar, than we need to consider my original proposal

*of establishing a new interest-free currency that can be
backed by gold, so inflation is controlled and the economy
is stabilized. The national debt would no longer be a threat
to our national security as all bills and expenses to operate
the nation, including operating the military would be paid
for with an interest-free currency that is backed by gold
and issued directly from the Treasury Secretary and not by
any central bank, like the tyrannical Federal Reserve
System. We must restore our currency with values, so
Americans can benefit off a more prosperous currency that
can literally guarantee more employment, reduction of
prices of goods, and a restrained government & central
bank that may not always have our "best interests" in their
hands. Every banking institution is corrupt; and
government is capable of being corrupt, when the two mix
together, they become a powerful weapon that endangers
our liberties and democracy. If they can get away with it,
with a smile on their face, while seeing millions of
Americans homeless and starving on the street, believe me,
they would and they would repeat they're their same
agenda just to benefit theirs.*

*Note: The Enlightened Party, in the meantime, while
plans are constructed to begin proposing legislation to
Congress to establish a new interest-free currency,
restoring our current "Federal Reserve Notes," to the
gold standard is not requested but demanded; until the
time comes, where the Federal Reserve System can be*

abolished and a new currency can and will replace it with
a fair and a more generous one, interest-free.

-Free electricity to all American households, to all
Americans in general in the United States of America-

There is one country on Earth, Libya, which grants free
electricity to all of its citizens; yet the United States of
America condemns Libya every day for its abuse of power,
similar to Syria. Nonetheless, free electricity is given to
every single citizen in that country. Why are we not
following this example? Electricity is an unlimited
resources, and that resources cannot vanquish on Earth. It
brings ultimate benefits to mankind, and if we're to
continue to be the most prosperous and advanced nation on
Earth, we need to consider generosity to the American
people. If electricity was not an unlimited resource on
Earth and has to be artificially made in order to take
advantage of its benefits, then the Enlightened Party would
never consider making a suggestion or proposal for it to be
free. But because, electricity has been on Earth since
Earth's existence, why are we taxing American citizens to
use its glorious gift when humans are not the ones who
make or produce electricity, when in fact, it is the Earth
that does. Most households in America, who have electric
bills, are few hundred to several hundred dollars, and will
continue to rise because municipal cities must find an
alternative to cover the costs and expenses of operating

*their city. But there will always be alternatives to paying
off the city's debt and operating expenses, besides charging
electricity, its called coming up with new brilliant
resolutions from creative politicians. Charging electricity
to Americans is yet another tax; and it is ridiculous
because, we already pay so many other taxes in addition to
having to pay for electricity. Not only that, but how can we
be declared a nation who represents equality, generosity,
and liberty, when some household occupants have
electricity because those occupants can afford it, and some
households with occupants do not have electricity, because
those occupants cannot afford it? This is a division of our
nation between the very less-fortunate, and the rich; as I
can no longer mention the existence of the middle-class,
becausese it no longer exists in America, as its existence
has been utterly destroyed by both the Democratic Party
and the Republican Party. It's so sad and disappointing to
realize and yet still not understand why some Americans
are going to sleep everynight without electricity to warm
them during the days that bring cold weather, and how
some children are forced to eat cold meals because the
child's parents or guardians cannot afford electricity to
operate the microwave, or just as equally bad, is the idea
that food will inevitably spoil in a refrigerator that does
function because of lack of electricity. Municipal cities are
treating electricity as if its a luxury like a cell phone.
Electricity is produced from the Earth, cellular phones are*

manufactured and invented by human-beings. There's a big difference between the two! If the American government can allow poverty to increase to the point where some Americans are surviving without electricity, while others are surviving with it, then we still have not completely evolved as a nation when compared to previous decades and centuries in the United States. Candle-lit dinners are not a bad thing, if its for a night or two of relaxation, or for a romantic dinner with a significant other, but to survive every day without electricity is certainly not tolerated or acceptable by the Enlightened Party. The Enlightened Party supports a bill or an Amendment that requires all American households in the United States of America to have free electricity in their households, regardless of low, average, or high income. This is about equality, and not division. The Enlightened Party, with its representatives, upon being elected in Congress, will see this agenda as one of the top priorities to accomplish as it's essential and necessary to provide our citizens with the resources that they need to survive with. The American people deserve this, and any opposition to this idea from any city, state, and the federal government, and any political party are from entities that do not care to see the struggle and sacrifices of the American people to end. The Enlightened Party does care for this struggle and sacrifice to be exterminated immediately.

*-Free Internet to all American households, to all Americans
in general-*

*The 21ˢᵗ century is a century of elevated technology and is
definitely a global transformation and manifestation of
higher consciousness and the willing determination for
mankind to excel in advanced technology. This is a good
thing; as we can begin to recognize & realize that mankind
is currently at a stage, where the transition from obtaining
information through efforts of persistent research is
available through the internet, which is the second and only
other alternative to reading books at a library or
purchasing books at a bookstore. The internet has so much
essential and important information & knowledge that
allows American citizens to learn quickly and do more
research conveniently & effectively. It's the truth! The
internet has created millions of jobs for Americans, and the
internet has also given us a more convenient lifestyle where
paying bills online can be done, rather than driving to the
gas company to pay your bill or the post office to get a
money order to pay your rent. The internet can also help
you find your new home, if you do extensive & adequate
research on locating the home that fits your needs. You can
almost do anything on the internet; but it always come with
a price; as do all great things. On average, most Americans
pay between $35.00-$100.00 to take advantage of the
beautiful opportunity of having the internet either on
they're their phone or on their computer at they're their*

residence. The internet can and will always offer great benefits and opportunities; but the Enlightened Party views the idea of not having "free internet to all American households," as a threat to our nation's economy. Almost all employers, with the exception of certain small businesses, (which is still small by the way) require candidates who are looking for a job at their business to apply on online, which obviously requires access to the internet. Some major corporations, (very few of them) have computers that are accessible at their business, while the majority of businesses don't. If you don't have access to the internet, the only other five options, with the exception of using your phone, (not always the best idea) are the following:

1. *Go to the public library*
2. *Go to your school's public library*
3. *Go to the unemployment office*
4. *Go and visit a friend, relative, and/or domestic partner to have access to they're their internet.*
5. *Go to a cafe or place of business that offers "free Wi-Fi."*

The Enlightened Party renders the outmost and sincere thanks to all the corporations and businesses who offer free internet at their place of business. These corporations

85

*and/or businesses could charge if they want to, but instead,
they offer a free service to mankind, that encourages
consumers to go to their place of business and remain there
as loyal customers, who will more than likely buy food
and/or merchandise at that same business and then take
advantage of their service of free internet. Obviously,
businesses and corporations have to pay for this service,
but they make up for it in massive revenue and profits that
are collected from consumers as a result of selling goods to
the public. But now it's time to take this a step further! The
Internet should not come with a price as a television does
or a laptop. Those are luxury items. Those are electronic
items that are fabulous inventions to possess, but in no way
does it compare to the internet. The internet operates today
through wireless signals broadcast all over the world,
although it was invented by man, through its system of
servers, the wireless signals in the air, provides all the
necessary work for humans to enjoy a pleasant internet
experience. The human-eye cannot see these signals, but it
exists in front of us like the air that we breathe everyday to
survive another day. It is a form of energy. First of all, the
Enlightened Party views the internet as a resolution that
can improve and stabilize our economy, through allowing
Americans to possess the internet at their households, so
Americans can properly and comfortably look for jobs, and
possibly start a business to create jobs. Another benefit to
having free internet to all households is the continued*

*ability for the United States to remain a super-power
nation through advanced technology and knowledge. If the
internet is available to all Americans, free-of-charge, the
possibility of an American doing "extensive research" to
gain proper knowledge and learn how to obtain proper &
essential resources to invent or discover something
beneficial to mankind is immenent, crucial, and necessary.
All it takes is a bright, articulate, & intelligent American,
with excessive persistence to see this happen, and the
possibility is always there.* **It's no longer a secret, that the
person who seeks and desires, will inevitably find what he
or she has been looking and waiting for.** *The internet
makes this easier and much more likely to happen. If this
were to happen, the United States of America will continue
to remain a superpower nation and excel & advance above
all other nations in terms of knowledge & wisdom, and
severe intelligence. America has always represented those
three words,* **knowledge, wisdom, and intelligence!** *But
now it's for the city, state & federal government to begin
issuing free internet to all Americans. We must be
compassionate and generous to those Americans who
cannot afford a decent wage to pay they're their internet
bill. As I mentioned before, we cannot be a nation of
generosity and compassion, if we allow only those
Americans who pay for their internet to have the internet;
while those struggling Americans who are struggling to
survive are without any internet in they're their household,*

*because they cannot afford it. This is absolutely wrong!
There are over 125 million households in the United States
of America as of 2016, electricity and the internet should
be free and available to each and every one of these
households, regardless of low, average, or high income
status. The Enlightened Party endorses and supports a bill
or an Amendment guaranteeing this right to each and every
American; and upon its representatives being elected in
Congress, will immediately submit proper legislation to see
that we change history for the better of Americans, which
they so rightfully deserve, have earned, and need.*

-Gay Marriage & LGBT rights-

*Homosexuality is a natural and normal feeling and thing. It
has existed for centuries and will continue to exist. It
should not even be a debate whether gay marriage should
be legal or not. The Enlightened Party supports same-sex
marriage and supports civil liberties and equality for LGBT
people. It is a moral and compassionate right and gratitude
for LGBT whose only desire in America is to excel in life,
and live in peace as all other Americans. When I hear of
the abusive practices that are inflicted upon by cowards
who harbor hatred against their fellow human-beings, just
because of they're their sexual orientation, it is
disappointing and immoral. Mankind must stick together in
order to prevent the threat of its own extinction, regardless
of race, gender, and sexual orientation. Everyday, our*

freedom of speech is protected from our military which consists of both straight and gay military-armed-forces members who protect this right for us, as well as the rest of our other rights that are guaranteed to every American, that are listed in the United States Constitution. How hypocritical we must be to want gay military-armed-forces members to protect our practices of the United States Constitution, and yet we will not want to protect their right to marry who they love and cherish! I am grateful every day to our military for what it provides to our great nation and its defense of all our civil liberties. Our Constitution only exists because of our military, not our government, our military ensures the protection of this, and the protectors of our Constitution include LGBT military-armed-forces members of all military branches. We must not also forget that LGBT in the civilian workforce, contribute to society by being law-abiding citizens, which includes paying taxes to they're their municipal, state, and federal government, every day, every month, and every year. They're their tax contributions which are required by law to collect from city, state, and federal governments, helps stimulate and preserve our economy. Therefore, they also provide a shield to our economy from debts and deficits as straight people do. We have many LGBT civilians who work in restaurants who make and serve us our food, and who take our orders from the menu at the drive-thru, or who process our groceries at the cash register at a supermarket, or who sell us our future homes, and also serve in government which helps to preserve and safeguard America's cities, states, and the nation itself. LGBT people have demonstrated outstanding leadership in both the civilian and military workforce; and still continue to do so; yet they are mistreated, primarily because religious-fanatics, are still trying to impose their religious beliefs that men and women are only meant to be or marry each other. No LGBT citizen in American, yet alone the world, should be mistreated or abused because of his or her actions and/or personality. The Enlightened Party is obliged to propose three resolutions (two bills and an Amendment) to help and protect all communities in the United States which consist of LGBT citizens.

1. *A Congressional Bill that prohibiting all employers in the United States of America not to discriminate based on sexual orientation, by refusing to hire that person because of his or her sexual orientation or transgender status (respectfully). In addition to this legislation, equal pay for LGBT people is required and should be the same as straight people, with the exception of work experience which may differ on each applicants work history, and also if the employer specifically states that "additional compensation is apparent Iif the candidate has work experience in a related field pertaining to the job that he or she is applying for.*

2. *A Congressional Bill that fines anyone (if they're properly convicted after being charged) discriminating or verbally abusing anyone who is LGBT in the United States of America by a minimum of $5,000, and if a second time occurs by the same offender, a jail sentence of a minimum of six months at a county jail, in addition to a fine of $10,000 is mandatory and required. If a third offense is repeated by the same offender, three years minimum in a federal prison will be mandatory in addition to a $50,000 fine. This sounds harsh, but the law needs to be harsh on bullies (religious- fanatics) who will do what they desire and want in order to offend innocent (LGBT) people based on they're their sexual orientation. People who will bully or persecute LGBT citizens do not deserve leniency or any form of clemency, as those offenders are trying to take away their civil liberties and practices which are guaranteed by the United States Constitution.*

3. *An Amendment to the United States Constitution granting, allowing, and recognizing Same-Sex marriages in the continental United States, and within all its territories and borders, stating that: "Marriage between a man and a woman, and between two men, and between two women, are and*

shall remain legal in all territories of the United
States of America."

We must do more for the LGBT community, as they're just
like the average and ordinary American who seeks the
American dream (a great paying job and the ability to
purchase a great residence), they are people with feelings
too and must be appreciated and cherished as straight
human-beings. To not do this, is unpatriotic and immoral.
If we want to continue to represent our nation as the nation
of fairness & equality, we must as Americans, first
recognize our potential and opportunity to always continue
the representation of our nation as liberty and justice for
all, by protecting and defending LGBT citizens, as they're
just like straight humans, only with different agendas and
goals. That's the only difference. There are no other
differences as we all have the same color of blood and the
same internal organs that exist in our immune system.

-Requiring the President & the Vice President of the United
States of America to have military service on their
background as a requirement to run for the office of the
President of the United States & the office of the Vice
President of the United States-

Out of 45 U.S. Presidents, including the newly-elected
President for the 2016 election, regardless whether it's

*Donald Trump or Hillary Clinton who gets elected as
President, only 32 have served in either the armed forces
and/or state militias. Throughout American history,
enlisting in the military was literally more easier than
breathing in oxygen. There were no obstacles and barriers,
as all you needed was half a brain (not to imply that former
veterans were stupid or incompetent) and a pulse. If you
had both of those criterias, you qualified and were eligible.
Over the years and the decades, regardless of the wars that
the United States has involved themselves in, enlisting in
any of the United States military branches, (Army, Marines,
Navy, Air Force, and Coast Guard) has become more
difficult and complicated. It shouldn't be this way, and this
national security issue should be resolved by the very same
government who we elect to represent us. There is more of
a chance to get disqualified from enlisting in any military
branch than at any point or time in the history of our great
country. So much to the point, that 5 out of every six
recruits are being rejected and denied military service from
the Military Entrance Processing Station (MEPS). I am no
fan of MEPS, and totally support the abolishment of that
department within the Department of Defense; and not the
Department of Defense itself. But, we will discuss the
reasons and necessities for abolishing MEPS on a different
topic. As I have stated, Americans that desire to serve their
country are being turned away by the state (National
Guard and Air National Guard) and federal (Army,*

Marines, Navy, Coast Guard, and Air Force) government. Contrary to what some people may assume or think, both enlisted and reserve military personell do not make a lot of money serving. While active-duty military personnel do receive outstanding benefits such as medical, dental, tuition assistance, the post 9/11 GI-Bill, and life insurance, in addition to paid vacation, this is far from a life of luxury and being well-off. Where am I getting at with this, you're probably wondering? Well, let us take a look at some comparisons between an enlisted Army soldier and the President of the United States.

Army Soldier Annual Salary & benefits: $18,804 (as an E-1 active-duty soldier in 2016) in addition to medical and dental benefits, post 9/11 GI-Bill, life insurance, and paid vacation, and retirement benefits; and basic housing allowance for dependents.

The President of the United States Salary & benefits: $400,000 (as of 2016) in addition to a $50,000 annual expense account, a $100,000 non-taxable travel-expense account, and $19,000 for entertainment expenses. That's more than half a million dollars that the U.S. President gets each year. The U.S. President also receives great medical benefits through The "Federal Employee Health Insurance Program" and although, the President is required in some cases to pay out-of-pocket expenses for medical treatment, the President gets free medical treatment within the White

House Premises and its territory through medical staff that are always available inside the White House for all emergency purposes. There really are no limits as to how much money the U.S. President receives from taxpayers for vacation purposes. President Obama has spent over 70 million dollars of taxpayer money to fund his vacations in both of his presidential terms combined. It's the truth. An enlisted Army soldier, depending on his or her rank and time-in-service, would receive between $1567.00 (E-1 pay with the most time-in-service)-$7683.00 (E-9 pay with the most time-in-service) a month, and only one month of paid vacation, since armed forces members are only eligible for 30 days a year paid-vacation. Compare that to half a million, is that really a lot?

Requirements to Join any of the five armed forces branches?

1. *U.S. citizen, or permanent resident in the United States, or have an active green-card that is valid.*
2. *Have a crime-free record (if you don't have one, you will need waivers which can always and easily be rejected).*
3. *Have a High School Diploma or a GED (General Education Development) with 15 college credits that's over a 100 college level.*

4. *Be at least 17 years of age with parental consent,
   all the way up to 35 years the max, although less in
   some military branches.*
5. *Be willing to defend and support the U.S.
   Constitution from all enemies foreign and domestic.*
6. *Be willing to sacrifice your life for your country, if
   and when it is necessary.*
7. *Successfully pass the ASVAB Test (Armed Forces
   Vocational Aptitude Battery) and get an AFQT
   between 32 (the Army)-50 (all the other remaining
   military branches), although, as of 2016, most
   recruiters will gladly turn away your application if
   you get below a 50.*
8. *Pass a full medical examination; which isn't always
   easy by the way.*
9. *You can't have too many dependents.*
10. *Have outstanding credit.*

*Those are a lot of requirements just to serve and defend
your country right? Do you really think all of these
requirements will always protect our Constitution and
national security, and our economy as a nation? We will
never remain the United States of America as long as we
have all of these requirements and regulations just to enlist
in the armed forces, not to mention as we cannot forget the
additional regulations that are listed by the Department of*

*Defense through MEPS. It's unbelievable and irresponsible
for our government to continue to allow all of these
regulations. It will regret all of these regulations the day
our great nation gets invaded by a domestic or foreign
enemy, and we cannot defend ourselves because of our low
supply of military forces, when we could have had a high
supply of military forces, but turned down many potential
armed forces members, despite they're their adequate
qualifications. This is definitely a national security issue.
Nothing is more dangerous or a threat to our nation than
all of these regulations. We need to go back to the days
where it's more easier and less complicated to enlist in the
armed forces.*

*Requirements to become President of the United States of
America:*

1. *Be a U.S. citizen.*
2. *Be 35 years of age.*
3. *Be 14 years a resident of the United States of
   America (which doesn't have to be consecutive).*
4. *Get Votes.*

*If you really think about it, does it not seem easier to run
for the office of the President of the United States of
America, and become a candidate for an upcoming
presidential election, than become a candidate to enlist in
the armed forces and enlist in the military? If a*

Presidential candidate decides to run for President or is in the beginning stages of declaring and opening an exploratory committee (to test the waters), then all that is needed to become an automatic candidate as a presidential candidate is raise more than $5,000 for a campaign. That sounds easy doesn't it? Keep in mind, the President is the Commander-In-Chief of all America's military branches, the President is above all of the highest-ranking generals in all of the armed forces. The President has the unconditional authority, to send our armed forces members into battle with or without a declaration of war from Congress, although Congress is supposed to declare war first before the President sends our armed forces members to war, but realistically speaking, asking Congress to declare war has not happened since World War II. Airstrikes and bombing other nations are acts of war, and since Congress has not authorized a formal declaration of war against a "specific nation" in general, as a nation, it is a violation of our Constitution to be conducting air strikes against other nations and bombing them without a proper declaration of war. The President of the United States authorizes these air strikes and bombings with or without getting approval from Congress which then demands and expects members of all of our armed forces to participate in these unconstitutional raids and invasions against other nations who never invaded our nation or threatened our nations national security. I find it unfortunate and pathetic

how one person, and only one person whose in charge of
our military, (the President of the United States of America)
can dictate our entire military, and override any
recommendations and proposals from our highest-ranking
generals in terms of appropriating resolutions and
measures to conquer and destroy the enemy, while the
President does not have to have military service on his or
her background. How is this possible? Why is this legal?
Let us take a look at the definition of Commander-In-Chief,
and for what it actually stands for and represents:

"The supreme commander of the armed forces of a nation,
or sometimes of several allied nations. An officer in
command of a particular portion of an armed force who
has been given this title by specific authorization." - The
Definition of Commander-In-Chief in almost all
dictionaries

Votes, or delegates, is what gives the President "specific
authorization" to be in charge of our military. A
Commander-In-Chief should have military experience on
his or her background, to understand how the military
works and operates, and to render his or her opinions,
which can contribute to a decisive victory against a
potential threat or enemy from within our outside of our
nation. While advice and recommendations from high-
ranking generals should be taken into some consideration,
depending on the circumstances, a President must execute

*a decision based on his or her own conscious, and this
requires discipline, which is what the military teaches to all
recruits beginning on the first day of basic training;
regardless of the selected military branch. It's time this
great nation of ours begins electing men and women for the
office of the President of the United States of America to
have military service on his or her background. It makes no
common-sense to allow a chicken-hawk who has
intentionally avoided military service during times of war,
or times of peace, to be in charge of our military and send
precious and sacred Americans into battle, to go to war. To
me, this is no different than allowing a cashier who has no
manager experience to run a store, without receiving any
manager training or ever having experience of being a
manager. This would offend many people; and I'm sure the
idea that a man or woman who has no military service in
his or her background, who is in charge of all our military
decisions, including armed forces members compensations
and benefits, can become President. It is outrageous and
irresponsible and yet another national security threat to
our nation to continue the process of allowing men and
women to run for President of the United States of America
who do not have military service on they're their
background. It is more inspirational and motivating for a
current enlisted, reserve, or officer in all of the armed
forces to know that that their president who occupies the
White House had once served in the military in an attempt*

to defend our great nation and uphold our sacred Constitution. I find it embarrassing and insulting to our military to hear presidential candidates speak on being a great "Commander-In-Chief" to our military, yet they know nothing about the military or how it feels to experience the harsh conditions of basic training which was a rejected alternative lifestyle, when compared to the majority of presidential candidates who decided to attend "Ivy-league" schools rather than first serve in the military and then attend college. Education is important, and I do not intend to dispute that. Speaking of education, did you know that you can run for President without having any high school diploma or GED? You certainly do not need 15 college credits to file any papers to the Federal Elections Commission to run for President. You certainly do not need to take a written examination consisting of mathematic, vocabulary, reading comprehension, science, mechanical, tests to be considered or eligible to run for President. You do not have to do take or receive a medical examination that consists of a vision test, hearing test, urine test, blood test, prostate-cancer test, color-blind test, and a multiple-exercise test (including the infamous duck-walk) from the Department of Defense and pass in order to become President of the United States. Why do military personnel have to take all of these tests to qualify to serve and defend their nation, when in fact they do defend our nation, much more than a President can do or accomplish; considering the President is not the one fighting during war, it's his or her members of the armed forces who are the ones fighting to preserve our democracy and Constitution? Shouldn't it be the other way around? Shouldn't the President have to take an ASVAB examination and full & thorough medical examination, after all, isn't the President the highest & supreme authority of all our military branches? If the President of the United States of America has the fate and destiny of America within his or her hands, should not the President demonstrate his or her ability to understand, comprehend, and pass the same subject-tests which are required for Americans who attempt to enlist in the armed forces? I can never support, nor will my political party, and its members ever support the notion or idea, that a President can represent and be in charge of all of our military branches and have no experience or understanding of how our military works and operates. The military teaches the ultimate method and practice of self-reliance, discipline, organization, and how to react in the most devastating and catastrophic events and circumstances, all of which can never be retrieved at any ivy-league school or civilian and/or government work-atmospheres. It is not impressive or patriotic, yet alone charismatic to have a President send precious and sacred Americans to war when the President him or herself, had the opportunity to go serve in the military during peace or war time, and refused to do so, especially when the President or presidential

candidates have avoided "drafts," by citing excuses as
being medically disqualified, when in fact, the President
and/or the presidential candidates have participated in
sports at their selected ivy-league school and excelled in
their desired sport. There's absolutely no excuse or way to
make up for this deception and cowardice to the American
people. I would encourage more current active-duty,
reserve, and officers in all of the military branches to begin
supporting the idea of requiring the President to whom they
(the people) elect by their votes for which they fight to
maintain to preserve democracy, to have military service
on his or her background. How patriotic, inspiring,
motivating, and charismatic will be the President who has
military service behind his or her background, and sends
precious and sacred Americans to war, and he or she leads
us leads us in every way, the way a "true" Commander-In-
Chief does to his military. With the ultimate and deepest
respect for the highest-ranking generals and/or admirals
who defend our nation every day, and who are experienced
at the highest of what they do and accomplish, I do believe
their opinions do matter. But their opinions do not matter
above a "true" Commander-In-Chief. A Commander-In-
Chief, who him or herself has served in the military and
demonstrated impeccable leadership that manifested into a
great award of an "honorable discharge." The Enlightened
Party, upon its representatives and/or senators being
elected into Congress, will begin drafting and proposing a

Bill or an Amendment to our Constitution to "Amend" Section 1, Article 2 of our sacred Constitution which shall state the following:

"No person except a natural born Citizen, or a Citizen of the United States, at the time of the Adoption of this Constitution, shall be eligible to the Office of President; neither shall any person be eligible to that Office who shall not have attained to the Age of thirty-five years, and been fourteen Years a resident within the United States, and has not served in any of the United States military branches while receiving an honorable discharge upon exiting from the selected military branch."

-The Second Amendment-

"A well regulated Militia, being necessary to the security of a free State, the right of the people to keep and bear Arms, shall not be infringed." - The 2nd Amendment to the United States Constitution.

The 2nd amendment was established by our founding fathers for one reason only! Because, the dangers and tyrannical threat from a government is more likely than any terrorist group or terrorist organization that is foreign or domestic. This includes governments that are Monarchy based, dictatorial based, Communist based, and especially Democracy based. The federal government in any nation, can easily convince and manipulate the general population

104

to believe that they're interested in helping them and the nation through reforms to improve the economy, decrease the unemployment rate, increase more civil liberties, raise the minimum wage, lower or abolish existing taxes for small businesses and corporations, and particularly in our great nation, uphold the United States Constitution. It's no secret that the Republican Party support the 2nd Amendment and the "right for Americans to keep and bear arms." While the Democratic Party, is known for its persistent and constant reputation of trampling over our Constitution and especially the 2nd Amendment. Democrats support gun control and discourage and oppose all members of Congress to issue any legislation that defends and upholds the right towards practicing the 2nd Amendment. Recent school shootings, street shootings, and even a theater shooting, have encouraged the federal government to issue more gun control resolutions towards these unfortunate events. However, I'm not convinced that all of these people who were convinced or killed in or after the process of killing innocent Americans were or currently are mentally ill. I am convinced that some were acting alone, and some were acting on behalf of the Central Intelligence Agency, and elements of the United States Government through bribery or mind control practices, to further elevate an agenda to destroy the 2nd Amendment from our Constitution. If the U.S. Government ever has the opportunity to take away our rights to own firearms, we

would be in danger of liberty, life, and the pursuit to
happiness. More than likely, Americans would and could be
forced into a new form of slavery or even executed to fulfill
a depopulation agenda already properly planned and set
into motion years in advanced by elements of the U.S.
Federal Government and corporate entities. Whether or not
this is true, we must as Americans, hold the possibility that
this could be possible. The Central Intelligence Agency
does not have our interests in mind and truly desire to
enslave the American population. It is a cruel and ruthless
agency that must be destroyed. Their system of "MK-Ultra"
(the ability to hypnotize American civilians to assassinate
and remove patriotic figures who oppose and reject the
status-quo established by ruthless tyrants within the
American government and corporations) has been in effect
for decades and has probably been responsible for unusual
and unsolved murders involving patriotic Americans who
"spoke too much" of the dangers of allowing our
government to take over our rights and civil liberties.
Going back to the discussion of the 2nd Amendment, if we
ever allow our government or any other government to
propose any legislation to permanently confiscate our
weapons, we can kiss our democracy goodbye, as well as
our Constitution. Our 2nd Amendment protects our first
Amendment right (the right to free speech and freedom of
the press; and to publish). If we do not have our 2nd
Amendment to protect our 1st Amendment right, the U.S.

*Government will proclaim and advocate to protect our 1st
Amendment rights, but it will be a bond and promise
destined to be broken and with it the public's increased
distrust of the U.S. Government. Government, even If it's
from a country that practices Democracy, should never be
trusted or given the supreme authority to "only have
firearms." It is dangerous to our civil liberties and a
danger to our nation in general. Let us take a closer look at
the founding fathers mentality and opinions of the right "to
keep and bear arms," and consider that these opinions bare
consistent truth and honor:*

*" A free people ought not only to be armed, but
disciplined." - George Washington (1st President of the
United States of America & Founding Father)*

*"What country can preserve its liberties if their rulers are
not warned from time to time that their people preserve the
spirit of resistance? Let them take arms!" - Thomas
Jefferson (3rd President of the United States of America &
Founding Father)*

*"The right of the people to keep and bear arms shall not be
infringed. A well regulated militia, composed of the body of
the people, trained to arms, is the best and most natural
defense of a free country." - James Madison (4th President
of the United States of America, Founding Father, and
Father of the Constitution)*

"The Constitution shall never be construed to prevent the people of the United States who are peaceable citizens from keeping their own arms." - Samuel Adams (4th Governor of Massachusetts & Founding Father)

"For it is a truth, with the experience of ages has attested, that the people are always most in danger when the means of injuring their rights are in the possession of those of whom they entertain the least suspicion." - Alexander Hamilton (1st Secretary of the Treasury & Founding Father)

I am definitely going to take the word, opinions, and integrity of our Founding Fathers much more seriously than our current Democratic politicians who always try to dispel any rumor or theory that the government will become tyrannical once gun control is established and all firearms are confiscated and removed from all Americans, except members of the armed forces and law enforcement. We must never forget the consequences throughout history of what has happened to civilians of a nation, who allowed their government to confiscate their firearms, to provide them security at the expense of sacrificing their liberty to own a firearm. Inevitably, that system of government or nation became and naturally becomes tyrannical and begins suspending or destroying additional civil liberties first, then secondly, exterminating massive amounts of their country's population. There is no winner but evil and dictatorship. The only option to retrieve the right and

*liberty to have a firearm would be to establish a coup d'etat
and violent revolution which also consists of massive
depopulation through a civil war in that nation. The winner
is not necessarily the survivor, but the person who still has
the power and authority to make laws in that country with
or without support from that nations population. Let us
never forget these very own words (quotations) of these
notorious tyrants who define the very definition of the word
"serial killer:"*

*"The easiest way to gain control of a population is to carry
out acts of terror. The public will clamor for such laws if
their personal security is threatened." - Joseph Stalin
(banned the use of firearms to his citizens, and then
exterminated over 20 million of them, once they were
defenseless)*

*"Ideas are more powerful than guns. We should not let our
enemies have guns, why should we let them have ideas?".
- Joseph Stalin (banned the use of firearms to his citizens,
and then exterminated over 20 million Russian civilians,
once they were defenseless)*

*"All political power comes from the barrel of the gun. You
register and ban the firearms before the slaughter."
- Mao Tse Tung (banned the use of firearms to his citizens,
and then exterminated over 20 million Chinese civilians,
once they were defenseless)*

"To conquer a nation, first disarm its citizens."
- Adolf Hitler (banned the use of firearms to his citizens,
and then exterminated over 13 million German civilians,
once they were defenseless)

Let us never forget Thomas Jefferson's clear warning and
the potential threat of tyranny within a nation, particularly,
the United States of America:

"When the people fear the government, there is tyranny.
When the government fears the people, there is liberty."
- Thomas Jefferson (3rd President of the United States &
Founding Father)

Now, let us not forget the words from the worst president
that our nation has ever put to occupy the White House, a
President who will leave the Oval Office and America's
debt crisis at 20 trillion dollars; and is credited with
allowing banking and credit institutions to help bankrupt
our nation, these are the words form the tyrant himself,
which is an attempt to convince the population that the
threat of tyranny from the Founding Fathers, and current
patriotic Americans are nothing more but conspiracy
theories and should be completely rejected and ignored as
false, as America would or never could do such a thing:

"They'll warn that tyranny is always lurking just around the
corner. You should reject those voices."

*The Enlightened
Party Manifesto
(Its Principles &
Ideologies)*

*- Barack Hussein Obama (44th President of the United
States of America & tyrant)*

*"I don't believe people should be able to own guns."
- Barack Hussein Obama (44th President of the United
States of America & tyrant)*

***We cannot take any chances for the state and federal
government to propose and pass legislation that take away
our rights to own firearms****. If we give away our guns to
our government, we might as well sign our death certificate
and ask the government, when will we die? The United
States is already at a point in history where its being
credited as a nation of Oligarchy (a small group of people
having control of a country) instead of Democracy, or
Fascism (a merger of government and corporations that
decide the fate and destiny of the nation they occupy, in our
case, the United States of America) instead of Democracy.
Never-before, in the history of our nation, have the
American people distrusted and questioned their
government than they do today. Even during the great
depression, fate in the state and federal government was
more stronger and powerful than what it is today. People
love and enjoy a nation that practices Democracy, but are
disappointed to think and feel when the Republic that they
live in, is not representing the very definition of Democracy.
I believe that if any state and/or federal government
propose to confiscate or ban all firearms in this country,*

111

thus destroying our precious and sacred 2nd amendment, then we the people, should rise up as a militia, and defend ourselves from a government who is attempting to first enslave us, and then kill us. No, it will be the government and the military that defends their status-quo who will be annihilated and destroyed before that happens by we the people. In this case, sacrificing our lives to preserve Democracy as also Thomas Jefferson warned must be repeated time and time again, is essentially worth it, to promise our posterity the continued existence of a nation that continues to practice Democracy in their favor.

-A Congressional Bill to require the Veterans Affairs to cover the cost for a one-time-only down-payment of a maximum of $5,000 at participating dealerships that sell vehicles to veterans who can provide proof of their discharge from military service   .

&

To also require the Veterans Affairs to cover the cost of the down-payment regardless of insufficient credit status. This bill would also require all banks to approve all veterans of car loans, regardless of the status of credit of the veteran. The only exception to this rule is if the veteran does not have sufficient income to pay for the monthly payments which are required to pay off the vehicle over time-

It's no secret that other nations give more efficient and generous benefits to their armed forces members and veterans. It's also no secret that our veterans are constantly being mistreated by unprofessional staff at the Veterans Affairs who are supposed to be offering the best and respected care and service to our veterans. It's unfortunate; and what's also unfortunate is to hear from time and time again, that the military receives cuts in tuition-assistance (a benefit that pays for active-duty armed forces members to attend college during their enlistment in the military) or cuts in military branches by laying off armed forces members of their MOS (military occupational specialty) or demoting them because of severe budget cuts. This represents an utter complete disorganization within our state and federal government. Nowadays, its more common to hear our veterans have their benefits temporarily suspended or taken away permanently instead of receiving a new benefit or an extended benefit of some kind. It's embarrassing and an insult to the people who serve and defend our country. Is this the thanks that we give to them for sacrificing years and precious time of their lives, that they're never going to be able to get back from us? No, we cannot do this to our veterans, thanking them for their service is simply not enough, although it demonstrates a sense of gratitude and compassion. I cannot, and neither will my political party, for whom I represent and founded, to allow the continued rejection and denial of services and

*benefits to our patriotic members of all our armed forces
and veterans who have retired from the military, and who
have given their every effort and sacrifices, to receive an
"honorable discharge or a "general discharge" from their
military branch. The Democratic Party and the Republican
Party have and are currently responsible for the
deprivation of benefits and resources that are supposed to
be given to our military but is consistently rejected despite
that fact, that these veterans have earned these benefits and
resources and certainly deserve more than what Congress
currently offers them. It's unfortunate and a disgrace. Most
politicians in any political party will condemn this
treatment to our precious and sacred members of our
armed forces and veterans, but once those politicians are
elected, those politicians will do nothing to correct this
condemnation. They will tolerate it, they will accept it, and
they will break their promises to help our veterans, and will
more than likely vote against any proposed-bill to offer
members of the armed forces and our veterans more
benefits and resources. More distrust in Congress will
increase, and these same people will lie and lie again just
to get reelected while breaking more promises. The
American people only fall for it, because we are a forgiving
nation; and truly believe in more than just second chances,
which should only and always prove and demonstrate that
Americans are compassionate, selfless, and generous to
our fellow human-beings as we should always be;*

*regardless If people have betrayed, mistreated, or broken
their promises to us. Every human-being Is different and
comes with gifts and talents, and flaws. Nobody is designed
to be perfect and flawless. The best thing that we can do is
help our fellow species (mankind) elevate into something
better than what we are today. We must help our veterans
and never break our promises to them. We are still the
United States of America because of there they're their
endless sacrifices and devotion to our country and our
Constitution. I'm convinced today, more than in any time in
the history of our country, more veterans are homeless and
without proper benefits and resources from the federal
government that they rightfully deserve and have earned
through loyal service in our military. President Obama is a
laughing stock when it comes to him protecting and
supplying our military with tools and resources that they
need in order to guard pour nation from any terrorist
threats or invasions that are being engineered by tyrants in
and outside our nation. The United States has two enemies,
radical Islamic-extremists, some of which are working with
and for the Central Intelligence Agency, and some who are
going rogue, and the other enemies are the banking and
credit institutions that exist in our nation, particularly the
Federal Reserve System. I still find it ridiculous how the
Federal Reserve System and the Internal Revenue Service
taxes military personnel and veterans through inflation and
taxation, which is the very same people who protect and*

have protected their ability to operate as independent corporations and entities. In other words, the military protects the very same people who tax them of their hard-earned money. If the military really wanted to, it could wipe out all the Federal Reserve Banks and the Internal Revenue Service, but this would be act of war against our nation, and a form of terrorism, because the only terrorists who are allowed to operate legally in America and take away all our rights, while increasing their profits, and power over our country are bankers and politicians who are in bed with bankers and corporate tyrants. Anyway, I believe that no veteran, who has exited their military branch with dignity and respect, and who has received either a general discharge or honorable discharge, should be denied access to proper transportation. I believe a lot of veterans today use public transportation as a method of going towards desired destinations, and while public transportation is not a bad thing, as it is a great thing, I believe that veterans should have access to a vehicle of their choice, as any other American civilian or veteran. However, I am proposing a legislative bill that will require Congress to authorize the Department of Veteran Affairs to cover the cost of a down-payment that is required for a vehicle that the veteran is attempting to purchase at an authorized and operating dealership within all the territories that belong to the United States of America. Obviously, prices depend on the size and quality of the *vehicle, but I propose a maximum of $5,000 be given to the dealership to cover the cost of a down-payment requirement upfront. Generally for the most part, most people who attempt and successfully purchase vehicles at participating dealerships, if they (the people) have to pay a down-payment because that persons credit was not satisfactory or high enough to consider that consumer to not be a credit risk, and when and if this happens, most people will pay upfront the down-payment of an average of $1,500-$4,500 to qualify for the purchase of the vehicle through credit or leases. The truth is, the higher deposit that you pay upfront to the dealership, the lower the monthly payment will be to the consumer. This actually does save money to the consumer and of course the interest accumulated over time, depending on the contract that is given to the consumer by the dealership. However, we must look at the advantages of this proposed legislation that would do three great things.*

1. *It would give every single veteran and every future veteran of this country an opportunity to have reliable transportation, which has never been done before in the history of our country.*
2. *Since, more veterans would be encouraged and more than likely to purchase a vehicle (through credit) at a participating dealership, the dealerships would increase their business and profits and thus would generate more revenue for the auto industry,*

> *thus the auto industry would begin creating and
> establish more jobs in the job market, which would
> inevitably decrease the unemployment rate.*
> 3. *The increased purchases of vehicles by veterans at
>   a participating dealership, would inevitably
>   stimulate the economy.*

*Now, everything nice has to come with a price, right?
Indeed, nothing is free in life. Every-single-fantastic idea
and legislation that benefits the majority of an existing
population, comes with expenses that are paid for by the
federal government, at the sole discretion of the U.S.
Congress. Currently, there are about 22 million veterans in
the United States and that amount will continue to elevate
as fortunately as Americans live longer, and unfortunately
as potential or the threat of war(s) will require more
additional armed forces members to enlist based on the
necessities of unnecessary wars established by the infinite
war on terror.*

*22,000,000.00 (veterans)X$5,000.00 (the required vehicle
down-payment)=$11,000,000,000.00 (the cost of money the
U.S. government would have to pay to cover the costs of
these measures implemented)*

*Realistically speaking, even if this proposed legislation
passed over night and became effective the following day,*

118

22 million veterans would not go to a dealership and claim their vehicle of their choice. Although, they can, and it would definitely be encouraged for them to do so, the amount of eleven billion dollars to cover these costs is the highest amount that would cost to implement these measures. I only put the maximum portion as an example. First, some veterans will not be required to put down a down-payment because of their amazing credit-score. Secondly, some veterans can voluntarily put down a down-payment as well, even though some veterans qualify not do so based on outstanding credit. Third, for those veterans who are required to pay a down-payment based on insufficient credit, may not always be required to put a down-payment of $5,000 to qualify for the purchase of the vehicle. If the down payment of $2,5000 is required to qualify for the purchase (through credit) of the vehicle), then the U.S. government will not have to cover the remaining portion of the expenses of the vehicle through the down payment process. Fourthly, and to make this very clear, if a veteran qualifies for a down-payment of purchasing the vehicle at the dealership, and the minimum down-payment is $1,000 or $1,500, the veteran may only put the minimum-portion amount down to qualify (through credit) to purchase the vehicle, and whatever balance is left that does not exceed the $5,000, can be saved for another transaction to purchase another vehicle to cover another down-payment for another vehicle. However, the one-time-

*only process of purchasing a vehicle for the Veterans
Affairs to cover the down payment only applies towards
maximizing the $5,000 amount that is given to every
veteran. If there is any remaining balance left, the veterans
is more than welcome and legally allowed (and encouraged)
to apply the existing-remaining balance of the down
payment towards another vehicle at a participating
dealership. I think this generosity will help rehabilitate the
consistent governments attempt to deny and reject benefits
that our precious and sacred veterans and current members
of all of the armed forces have so rightfully earned and will
always deserve.*

**Note: This will not be the only proposed legislation to
increase and/or establish benefits and more opportunities
for our sacred veterans. There will be many proposed
legislations to elevate more benefits and to protect the
rights of our veterans, by banging the suspension of
benefits to our veterans; regardless of consistent failure
for Congress and the President of the United States to
compromise on a budget, involving our military and the
economy. This will not be tolerated or over condoned by
members of the Enlightened Party who serve their
honorable constituents. It will be a violation and
expulsion of our members to ever vote on a proposed
legislation to suspend, decrease, and terminate existing
benefits and resources to our military. This is a serious
offense and will not be tolerated by the founder, the party,**

and among our members, it is a disgrace and insult to our party, the American People, and our precious and sacred veterans. The Enlightened Party's agenda is to maintain this consistency of aiding and protecting our military and our veterans, always and forever, despite any opposition from elements in the federal government.

-Proposing to Amend the First Amendment by abolishing all religion and its practices in all the territories that belong to the United States of America-

I would be liar and a hypocrite if I denied the fact that I authored the "Enlightened Luciferian," which encourages two things & practices:

1. *The encouragement for all Americans to study and practice the doctrine of attraction into their own lives, and see for themselves the true results that it works.*
2. *The destruction and abolishment of all religions on Earth, including the United States of America.*

Naturally, I welcome and challenge any opposition to my attempt to destroy religion. I cannot defend religion or its mythological interpretations knowing that religions, including but not limited to Christianity, Catholicism, Judaism, and Islam, have all been responsible for depopulation of the human race, enslavement of the human race, deprivation of individual civil-liberties, evolution of

121

technology, through the constant intimidation of "playing
with God," to make essential discoveries and invent
powerful and useful technology and/or products, and
currently, as religion has always done throughout history,
make war to protect and defend its meaning and beliefs. Let
us make no mistake that religion has always involved itself
into politics, and still currently does. I have no doubt that
some (not all) members of the United States Congress,
including independent state legislatures, write and propose
and vote on legislations based on they're their religious
beliefs. Their religious belief constitutes the highest
authority to either pass or reject all forms of legislation;
with "political opinion," coming second, although it should
always be first. I don't see this as moral, right, and fair. I
can give two political objectives or discussions that have
been challenged by politicians who put their religious
beliefs above their own political parties beliefs, or the
majority of the populations support for the controversy
surrounding a specific proposed legislation authorizing
and legalizing something that has never been legal or once
was legal, but no longer, or not currently legal.

1. *Gay Marriage has been challenged by members of*
   the United States Congress, particularly by
   members of the Republican Party, who see the
   institution of marriage between "one man and one
   woman." These beliefs are not derived from the
   United States Constitution, as they're derived from

*religious beliefs. These religious beliefs are from
the Old and the New Testament, and if there is a
Muslim member of Congress, more than likely, the
Muslim will follow the ideas and principles of the
Holy Quran which supports the same law or custom
that only a marriage between a man and a woman
should be legal, valid, and recognized by the federal
government. In this case, there is no separation of
church and state; for if there was, members of
Congress would vote and support gay marriage
because the majority of Americans do. But these
cowardly members of Congress, would rather deny
the rights and desires of the gay population, to save
him or herself from burning eternally in hell, for not
defending his or her religion and religious beliefs.
So, to save one soul from burning in hell, millions of
the LGBT population must be denied their rights
and civil liberties that are granted to heterosexual
couples and heterosexual people in general. I have
no mercy or compassion for members of the United
States Congress who are against gay marriage
because of their religious beliefs, as I can happily
express that these members of Congress don't
deserve to be politicians and do not deserve to have
any honor behind their name, to deprive civil
liberties to one group people (The LGBT*

*community), and grant civil liberties to another
group of people (the heterosexuals).*

2. *Planned Parenthood is another political
controversy that involves religious beliefs above
"political opinions." Some members of the United
States Congress oppose abortion, which is funded
by the federal and state governments to help in this
process. Some politicians claim that this constitutes
"murder" because a fetus is surviving in a womb of
a woman. For the most part, most Christians,
Judaists and Catholics, are pro-life and against
abortion. The majority of our politicians are from
these three religions. However, I will say that there
are some members of the U.S. Congress who are
religious, but who will place their religious beliefs
aside or behind them, and put the public's support
first, which is what should be done but is not
currently being done by members of the U.S.
Congress.*

*Currently, the First Amendment in the United States
Constitution states that:*

*"Congress shall make no law, respecting an establishment
of religion, or prohibiting the free exercise thereof; or
abridging the freedom of speech, or of the press; or of the*

right of the people peaceably to assemble, and to petition
the government for a redress of grievances."   *- First*
Amendment (United States Constitution)

First and foremost, The Enlightened Party is and will be
the only political party in the United States who believes in
freedom, liberty, and supports the idea of advanced
principles and technology in the United States of America
above all other nations. We will demonstrate and prove this
from time and time again to the American People, with
frequent legislation to maximize our civil liberties, and to
restrain government which must be restrained from
endangering our civil liberties. Secondly, when I propose
abolishing all forms of religion in America, I do not
propose, condone, or encourage the enslavement (by
throwing Americans into prison) of sacred Americans if
Americans refuse to give up their beliefs and religion. Only
a government who will enforce this with the aid and
support of a military can accomplish this, with a consistent
threat of warning of the potential consequences for anyone
who purchase religious icons or symbols and hangs them
out their doorstep or place these on their automobiles, or at
their work environment; like a Communist country is
known for doing. I cannot support a full-force of any
government arresting or enslaving people because of a
person attempting to practice his or her beliefs. However,
when I propose abolishing all forms of religion in America,
I do support three things, and will continue proper

125

*legislation regardless of intense opposition and barriers
from the general population or from members of the U.S.
Congress, because of religious history. These are my three
ideas to gradually destroy all religions in America:*

1. *Ban the sales of all religious icon (Crucifixes) and
   religious books (Holy Bible, Holy Quran, and any
   other religious book and the Satanic Bible), in
   America.*
2. *Remove anything (statues or monuments) that
   symbolizes any form of religion, or is derived or
   established as a monument or statue from verses or
   texts from a book that represents a specific religion.*
3. *Close down every church, mosque, and place of
   worship, including the Satanic Church, in all
   territories and borders that belong to the United
   States of America.*

*I do not support arresting anyone who practices their
religious belief, unless it's a way to recruit terrorism to go
against the United States Federal Government like radical
Muslims are currently trying to do. If people want to keep
their religious icons and books, and decide to practice their
religious beliefs inside their home, that should be legal and
recognized. However, the Enlightened Party cannot*

support or condone the frequent sale of a book (The Holy
Bible) that does three things of many more things.

1. Kill (stone) unbelievers & heretics
2. Keep and make legal the practice of slavery
3. That women are inferior to men and must obey men
   at all times. (Maybe that's why some members of
   the U.S. Congress refuse to fight for equal pay for
   women)

Anyone who reads the Holy Bible and the Holy Quran, will
find the above three things that are mentioned within its
book. This is not humane and moral. This is preposterous
and truly contradicts the very definition of liberty and
freedom for which America has always stood for, and
currently stands for. I do support opening museums for
religions so people can study its history. However, I, in
addition to members of the Enlightened Party only support
the issuing pr printing of religious books in public and
school libraries only to educate an interested student in its
history. However, the sale of religious books and icons are
supported by this party to permanently be banned. Any
person caught selling these things to people should be cited
and punished according to law, as these same people are
allowing the sale of a religious belief to jeopardize civil
liberties for all Americans. For these reasons, and believe

me, I can state more reasons, upon being elected as a member of Congress, representing the Enlightened Party, I intend to issue a proposed Amendment to Amend the First Amend to the United States Constitution stating:

"Congress shall make no law respecting, recognizing and/or establishing any religion within the territories, jurisdictions, and borders of the United States, or prohibiting the free exercise thereof; or abridging the freedom of speech, or of the press, or the right of the people peaceably to assemble, and to petition the Government for a redress of grievances." - Proposed First Amendment to Amend our current First Amendment to the United States Constitution.

Note: the founder of the Enlightened Party is not an atheist, but does not recognize any religion, or identify himself to be part of any religious affiliation. Although, he has written the Enlightened Luciferian, thus supporting the Luciferian religion, if it is one, although this is being contested, as some Luciferians recognize the practice of Luciferianism as a belief or ideology rather than a religion. The author supports Luciferianism as a principle or ideology, but does not support any church of Lucifer or any religion that supports Luciferianism. Additionally, the founder has supported an idea for a Luciferian religion, however, the author and founder only supports a practice or belief of a religion that coexists

**with other religions, if the proposed Amendment to
Amend the Constitution is defeated. Additionally, if there
was ever a Luciferian religion, and the founder & author
was part of it in the future, to remove himself from being
label a hypocrite, the author and founder would sever all
ties with that religion and encourage the termination of
that religion if the proposed Amendment to Amend the
first Amendment in the Constitution reached to a point or
degree of consideration of actually being successful and
becoming a statute to the Constitution. Additionally,
Luciferianism is not an occult or satanic club or belief, as
I can admit and proudly come forward that Luciferian
principles and beliefs are derived and inspired from the
practice of the law of attraction.**

*-A proposed Amendment or Bill Abolishing all Political
Parties in all territories, jurisdictions, and borders, and the
participation of current existing political parties in all city,
state, and federal elections in the United States of America
(including the Enlightened Party to preserve and protect
Democracy)*

*As founder of this political party that was established for
the purpose of protecting and defending the American
People, through maximization of civil liberties, and
constraining the federal government, and from freeing
Americans from unnecessary debt that was inflicted upon
them by tyrants (bankers, creditors, & politicians), and for*

granting precious and sacred Americans with unlimited education, and the right for everyone to know and understand how to learn the law of attraction and apply to it they're their lives, and open a new business, and for our veterans to be able to get a vehicle to assist them in their transformation of becoming a civilian from a member of our armed forces. There are many many more. As, I can guarantee my supporters, my readers, and my enemies & objectors, this will not be the first book representing this political party, there will be several volumes with new ideas, from brilliant minds, all to accomplish three purposes, and three purposes only:

1. *To protect and preserve our endangered Democracy from terrorists; domestic and foreign, and within our government and our corporations.*
2. *To help and free (through ruthless debt) every American citizen, regardless of class or status of income, together, we're all the same*
3. *To restrain the government and keep it under control by the American People, and particularly by the Enlightened Party*

I can criticize and destroy political parties with my words, and convince the American people that political parties are morally, ethically, and ruthlessly not the solution or answer

*to preserving and defending both Democracy and the
American people. It is no longer a secret, (if it ever was)
that political parties always swear "oaths" to put the
American people first before parties, but time and time
again, this lie and insult to an oath taken has alwaysys
backfired on the American People. These "oath-breakers,"
have broken their promise to the American People, to put
their they're their needs, and expectations first, and have
ignored these expectations and needs by going against
these needs and expectations by putting the "interest" of the
party first. Those politicans who refuse to obey thier
masters in they're their political party will not be supported
in the next election by that political party; and as a result,
that politicians can kiss their political party career goodbye. My last political party affiliation belonged to the
Republican Party; although, I will never say that this is the
best political party; as I have no doubt that this political
party, along with the Democrats are the reason why our
conutry has defaulted and been inferior to other nations all
over the world, and the reason why our Democracy is in
danger and threatened every day. Our economy suffers
because of both parties, as they're in charge of stabilizing
and repairing our economy from the recession of 2007.
They have done little to nothing to removing the national
debt and burden for which we the people still face as a
crisis. A new Presidential Administration will not repair
our 20 trillion dollar national debt. President Obama*

entered the White House with $10.6 trillion dollars as our national debt. It is now 19 trillion dollars, that means within eight years of his failed and destructive presidency, he has increased the national debt by over 87%, with an added $9.34 trillion dollars to the national debt. How is this responsible and allowed? President Obama has literally bankrupt our nation, and added more national debt to our country than all the other 43 presidents in history, combined. How can one President do so much damage? We can thank the Democratic Party for their reckless spending and poor leadership; to lead our nation as a prosperous nation. We can also thank the Republican Party for starting the great recession to begin with; and doing nothing to stop the crisis that we face today. These political parties have destroyed the confidence and trust of the American People. A significant portion of Americans do not trust political parties because of the Democratic Party and the Republican Party; and for good reason too. Have we seen any improvements today when compared to previous generations and decades? Have we seen real progress? Is our currency devaluing while food prices go up simultaneously due to the inflation of our currency? Has the cost of living increased? Not even the greatest liar on Earth can deny these facts or convince the general population that this isn't true. Even worse, the cost of living is getting worse and its becoming more difficult to survive and be financially stable today than it was generations and *decades ago; and becoming an independent person able to survive with a decent income and a decent job without having to worry if you might have to still live with your parents (not always a bad thing) but most Americans prefer to be independent and survive on their own. I know whoever is reading this book, desires to survive on his or her own, and enjoys the practice and lifestyle of being free and independent. Being dependent on something or someone is not always a great thing, and to me, it's one of the very worst things in life due to unforeseen circumstances and transitions. Growing up, I use to appreciate and like the Democratic Party, I use to think that it was a party that protected and cared for the middle-class and for the poor. I also grew up thinking that the Republican Party only cared for the rich and elite. I was wrong about both of these opinions and beliefs. The Democratic Party has a reputation of allowing banking institutions to run our nation ruthlessly (the Federal Reserve System) without auditing or challenging them, and the Republican Party has the same problem; allowing banking institutions and corporations to dictate and decide our domestic and foreign policies as if this was a Fascist nation. First of all, I'm surprised that the Democratic Party is still a political party; considering its reputation of refusing to abolish slavery during and after the American civil war; you would think that if politicians and Americans wanted to outlaw the Confederate flag because of its "alleged" trace to racism, these same people would preach the word of abolishing the very same political party that defended the practice of slavery, since common perception and opinion is that the Confederate flag "symbolizes and represents slavery and racism," which is everything that the Democratic Party once stood for. Consider these The facts which are 100% accurate and pathetic:*

The 13th Amendment to the United States Constitution (the Amendment to abolish slavery) had 100% Republican support & only 23% Democratic Support.

The 14th Amendment to the United States Constitution (the Amendment to give citizenship to freed slaves) had 94% Republican support and 0% Democratic support.

The 15th Amendment to the United States Constitution (the Amendment to grant the right for every American the right to vote) had 100% Republican support and 0% Democratic support.

Let us not forget the founding of the Ku Klux Klan to aid and support the Democratic Party, as it was founded by supporters of the Democratic Party. Its two main targets were freed African-Americans and Republican civilians and politicians. The ideology and beliefs of the KKK were to preserve and protect "White Supremacist beliefs" that the negro race were inferior to the white race; as Democratic politicians publicly and proudly announced in

134

Congress, to Congress, to Presidents, and to the American constituents. That's not to say that some Republican politicians did not believe in this false theory, although, those Republicans who did believe in this false theory, still did what was right and fought to establish more rights and equality for African Americans which should have been done since the founding of our nation. I do find it pathetic and embarrassing that it literally took sixteen presidents to literally free the slaves, even though we have only had 44 presidents (as the publication of this book despite a next presidential administration approaching next year in the United States in 2017), and have only been a nation for 240 years (after July 4th, 2016). As for the Affordable Care Act (Obamacare), which requires every American to purchase health insurance, regardless of income status, that tyrannical and ruthless measure successfully passed as a legal statute because of 86% Democrat support; with the Republican Party rendering 0% support for the passage of that bill. Currently, Obamacare is being challenged by the Republican Party and Supreme Court Justices because its original purpose and ideas regarding the bill, are not working. Health Insurance premiums are skyrocketing, deductibles are likewise also increasing, and some doctors will not even patients who are prescribed with Obamacare. But, again, this topic or discussion is for the abolishment of all political parties in America, and although, Democrats are attempting to grant affordable health insurance to most *if not all Americans, can never rebuild its reputation for defending and preserving slavery for decades and generations and for the entire 19th century, as well as portions of the 20th century. Currently, the Democratic Party has been able to fool and manipulate some Americans that their party is for the less fortunate and the middle-class, by proving this, the Democratic Party preaches and demands the elevation of the minimum wage in the United States, unemployment-compensation-extended benefits, fee-waivers & pell-grants for college, food stamps for the less fortunate, granting licenses or food stamps to immigrants, among others. The Republican Party is the exact opposite. The Republican Party, at least its beliefs and ideology believe that every person is responsible for his or her life, unless that person has severe mental or physical disability in which impairs him or her from surviving and doing essential duties that are otherwise practiced by the majority of Americans. The Republican Party is known for the encouragement of establishing and creating jobs for Americans by cutting taxes for small and large busineness's, which almost always becomes a misconception from the Dmeocratic Party, that the Republican Party is for the wealthy and elite class. I can agree that some members of the Republican party, including former Republican Presidents, and Vice Presidents, were and are still more interested in increasing their profits instead of helping the American People. The*

Republican Party also believes in a restrained government, and supports the idea for states to enact legislation that best fits the state that is attempting to implement a legislation to benefit that state. The Democratic Party believes in a large government to run and control our lives in case individual states fail to deliver on certain benefits and civil-liberties to Americans living in those states. The idea for the Republican Party to support individual states to make their own decisions on how to best lead their state in a prosperous and economical matter, is called **competition.** *In a way, we can think of individual states competing against other states like several competing businesses who sell the same merchandise and desire more consumers to come and remain loyal to a selected business. The idea that one state is more convenient and easier to live and raise a family, while get a decent living-wage and able to obtain a decent job from an employer depends on the leadership from the politicians who are hold elected offices in those states. For example, the cost-of-living in the state of New York and California are among the highest in the United States when compared to other states. It's not because of the massive population within those states, its becausese of failed leadership and the lack of ideas and talent to properly author a bill and submit it for consideration of passage through the state legislators.* **There's absolutely no reason or excuse why a one-bedroom apartment with one bathroom, in a terrible and**

**crime-infested neighborhood in the United States of
America, should cost three-four weeks of full-time work
that has been earned by the consumer! This is another
form of slavery and it must be stopped and addressed by
patriotic politicians with bright ideas to destroy this
unnecessary deduction from American wages who barely
survive paycheck-to-paycheck as it is.** *So, to counter this
national crisis (as it is not just in California and New York),
the Democratic Party has render their support for Section
8 housing which inevitably raises taxes for all hard
working Americans who are able to live without requiring
Section 8 assistance from the state and federal government.
Again, form time and time again, the Democratic Party has
proven their allegiance to helping the less fortunate by
supporting Section 8 housing for the less fortunate. Well, if
the Democratic Party really did care for the less fortunate,
why don't any of its members who occupy positions as state
legislatures or who occupy Congress, or even the
Democratic President himself, Barack Obama do
something about this skyrocketing-rent-epidemic-crisis that
is plaguing our nation and enslaving the majority of the
American People? The answer is because the Democratic
Party, along with the Republican Party, are both at fault at
this because both parties have put their parties interests
first, before the American people. So long as these political
parties continue to exist, and run our nation, the poison
from their leadership will slowly kill our nation; as there*

*will never be an antidote to cure our nation from the poison
that these ruthless and tyrannical political parties spit on
the American People, just to get elected, and promise
nothing to the American People, but disappointment and
betrayal. What the Republican party is today, is how the
Democratic Party was in the 19th century, and parts of the
20th century. In the 19th century, the Democratic Party
supported states rights, individual responsibility, and a
restrained government, and did not support benefits to a
selected class of citizens (African-Americans in particular),
while the Republican party in the 19th century and portions
of the 20th century, believe and support in almost
everything that the Democratic Party supports and
endorses today. In other words, the Republican Party in the
21st century is like the Democratic Party in the 19th century
and portions of the 20th century, and the Republican Party
in the 19th century and portions of the 20th century is like
the Democratic Party in the 21st century. I often wonder
why these political parties have changed their political
objectives and beliefs. The only plausible answer I can
think of is because these political parties desires to get
elected, and the only way to get elected is to adapt to
modern times, regardless of conservative beliefs and
ideologies. Two things for sure. One, the Great Depression
and the Great Recession of 2007, both happened during a
Republican-Presidential-Administration, (Herbert Hoover
& George W. Bush) and our national debt crisis of 19*

trillion dollars has been credited to a Democratic-Presidential-Administration (Barack Obama), although President Bush left office with our nation of 10.6 trillion dollars in debt, President Obama more than doubled this debt, and will leave office at almost tripling this debt. If President Obama had a third presidential-term, he would succeed automatically at multiplying our national debt three times more than what President Bush left the national debt at, to the American people. That's not outstanding leadership, and this represents a failure of a president to think of a clear and capable defensive-approach (or offensive approach) to eliminate or shrink our national debt before our country faces another major recession and/or great depression, which would destroy our nation and reputation as a super-power nation. Perhaps, America's first and only President, George Washington was right when he warned the American People of the practice and power of political parties who can and will attempt to usurp and deceive their constituents with failed promises and persistent deception without remorse and mercy.

"However, political parties may now and then answer popular ends, they are likely in the course of time and things, to become potent (influence) engines, by which cunning (deceitful), ambitious, and unprincipled men will be enabled to subvert (overthrow) the power of the people and to usurp for themselves the reins of government, destroying afterwards the very engines which have lifted

them to unjust dominion. - George Washington (1ˢᵗ
President of the United States & Founding Father)

Then, we have President John Adams, warning us about the
dangers of political parties which will inevitably attempt to
threaten our Democracy and our Constitution.

"There is nothing which I dread so much as a division of
the Republic into two great parties, each arranged under
its leader, and concerting measures in opposition to each
other. This, in my humble apprehension, is to be dreaded as
the greatest political evil under our Constitution."
- John Adams (2ⁿᵈ President of the United States &
Founding Father)

President John Adams belonged to the Federalist Party
(the first political party in the United States) and saw with
his very own eyes the potential & inevitable corruption of
political parties. President George Washington reminded
the American People of the dangers of political parties in
his farewell address, as he understood and knew that
political parties are manifested (created) to solve or fix a
few or several everlasting crisis that either endanger our
civil liberties, our economy, or our Constitution, or all of
the above.

"The alternate domination of one faction over another,
sharpened by the spirit of revenge, natural to party
dissension, which in different ages and countries has

*perpetrated the most horrid enormities, is itself a frightful
despotism. But this leads at length to a more formal and
permanent despotism. The disorders and miseries, which
result, gradually incline the minds of men to seek security
and repose in the absolute power of an individual; and
sooner or later the chief of some prevailing faction, more
able or more fortunate than his competitors, turns this
disposition to the purposes of his own elevation, on the
ruins of public liberty." - a portion of George Washington's
Farewell Address to the nation.*

*I cannot sit here and say that my political party offers and
brings the best solutions to the American people; I would
be biased and wrong if I said that, since the Enlightened
Party, with its ideologies and principles, desire and seek to
help the majority of Americans, which would be a threat to
certain wealthy-elites interests and way of life. All of these
principles and ideologies written in this book, came from
only one source, the author Simon Mark Alvarez. However,
as the party expands and grows, and welcomes the support
and endorsement of millions of Americans, more ideologies,
suggestions, recommendations, Bills, and Amendments will
be written and proposed by members of the Enlightened
Party, to support, defend, and liberate the American People,
through a prosperous economy, a chance to a decent and
elevating education, civil liberties for everyone, a powerful
currency (interest-free), and support the idea for every
American to learn how to build credit, and open a new*

*business, and just as importantly, to understand and
practice the law of attraction. Returning our current
currency to the gold standard to protect our currency and
prevent it from devaluing, while safe-guarding against
inflation, will always have the support and endorsement
from the Enlightened Party, as well as the support and
defense of our brave warriors and patriot's who have
sacrificed and continue to sacrifice their lives to defend
and protect our Democracy and Constitution. I desire with
my heart and soul to offer nothing but beneficial solutions
and resolutions to the American People, while aiding and
supporting every and any effort to destroy evil and ruthless
tyrants that operate within our state and federal
governments whose sole purpose is to enslave every
American just to increase their power and profits over the
American population. Make this no mistake, this is
happening right now in America, and perhaps, just perhaps,
my political party is the last one left to save our Democracy
and our Constitution before it is permanently destroyed by
these ruthless and heartless tyrants. If we say and do
nothing about this now, we will look forward to the future
with regrets and will begin to think to ourselves, "if only, I
could turn back the clock and go back in time, to give my
child a better future, when I had that chance and
opportunity?' It's not too late, and we must rise and stick
together, and if necessary, raise our own militia to demand
from the state and federal government our civil-rights and*

143

demands which will no doubt benefit the majority of the American people. If my political party were to be authorized and recognized by every state government, as well as the federal government, my political party would be the 55ᵗʰ politicval party designed and established to bring new principles and ideologies to the 21ˢᵗ century. As much as I can say that I wish my political party can exist forever electing the same patriotic and brave men and women to honorably and honestly serve our constituents for future centuries to come, I would be living in LaLa land, if I can think to myself that this can happen. I know that soon after I experience death along with people in my political party to whom I will serve with, and with future different generations to come, it will only be a matter of time until the Enlightened Party becomes distant and separated from its original intentions, principles, and ideologies. Because of this inevitable and potential threat, as I wish that this never happens, but nonetheless, the American People must be prepared for any sudden political party transformations as we have seen with both teh Democratic Party and the Republican Party. To counter this existing threat, I have personally written a Code of Conduct for all members who are affiliated with the Enlightened Party and who represent American constituents in all city, state, and federal elections to follow the code of conduct, or be expelled permanently from the Enlightened Party without any opportunity or chance to be affiliated with the Enlightened

*Party. My party will not tolerate deception and abusive
practices between members of the party, and against the
American people. I have written this Code of Conduct,
which can never be altered or deleted as a statute within
the Enlightened Party, as it can only be updated from time
to time by members of the party, its chairman, or the
founder upon 2/3rds of a popular vote within the party at
its convention, or a specific place where votes are placed
and authorized by the Enlightened Party.*

-Code of Conduct-

*All elected members of the Enlightened Party of
city, state, and federal offices within the territories,
jurisdictions, and borders that belong to the
United States of America, upon swearing in as an
newly or reelected members affiliated,
representing, and belonging to the Enlightened
Party, will swear an oath, placing their left hand
on the "Enlightened Party Manifesto, its principles
and ideologies," (of either volume), and raising
their right hand, while say the following oath:*

*"I, (state your name), will support, defend, and
protect the United States Constitution, Democracy,
and put my constituents interests first, before the*

*The Enlightened
Party Manifesto
(Its Principles &
Ideologies)*

*Enlightened Party's interests. I will faithfully,
honorably, and ethically bring forth legislation for
debate and consideration, that will benefit the
majority of an existing population, instead of
proposing legislation, which will benefit a small
portion of powerful elites. I will not accept or
receive any bribes, and will not work with
lobbyists or become a lobbyist, and will never
receive any contributions or donations from any
existing and practicing banking institution in the
United States, either as an elected official, or
running for office as an affiliated member of the
Enlightened Party. I will not abuse my authority
and take advantage of the American people, and I
will be required to resign from being a member
and affiliation of the Enlightened Party, if any
evidence is put forth by the American People, or by
members of the Enlightened Party against me
suggesting these violations, for in which case, I
shall have a right to an attorney to defend myself
against such accusations, and if found innocent, I
shall remain a member of the Enlightened Party,
at my own discretion. I will also agree and support*

146

*term limits for Congress and for the office of the
Presidency of the United States, in which case, I
shall follow the ideas for term limits for Congress
and as President, in which case, I shall be limited
towards running for reelections, while being a
member of the Enlightened Party. I will also never
reveal or share secrets that are essential and
important to the party, to other non-members or
rival parties, so long as I am a member, and so
long as I live... I swear as a member of the
Enlightened Party...*

*The person administering the oath shall be the founder, a
chairman, or a regular member of the Enlightened Party. A
copy of the oath will be at the convention, or a specific
place where members of the Enlightened Party may meet to
discuss ideas or suggestions for proposed legislation
and/or vote on a particular measure or support of a
measure. The location of these places will be revealed in
the near future. I would like to personally thank everyone
who read this book, regardless, if you take these ideas
seriously or not, or support them or not. Your time is
valuable and important to me and to the party. Your
interest in politics is also essential and important and
demonstrates your capability and interest to help make this
world a better place for ourselves and our posterity. I look*

147

*forward to writing a second and third volume to this book,
proposing new ideas and solutions to help make our
country safer and powerful again. The second volume will
consist of a real energy plan that the Enlightened Party
intends to put forth, as well as calling on the government to
establish a committee to investigate certain disturbances
and crisis in which our nation faces or will inevitably face,
among other new ideologies and principles. I look forward
to your support and endorsements, from you, the American.*

**Note: If the founder (Simon Mark Alvarez), or members
of his political party all of a sudden die suspiciously of
strange causes, just know that the founder is and has
never been suicidal, and enjoys and appreciates life. If I
die suddenly, after this book is released or die after my
political party is recognized, just know and remember
something; regardless of what the government says, my
death was no accident, and neither were the death of my
followers. The government killed us professionally;
despite its denial of being involved as either an
accomplice or the assassins themselves. - Simon Mark
Alvarez**

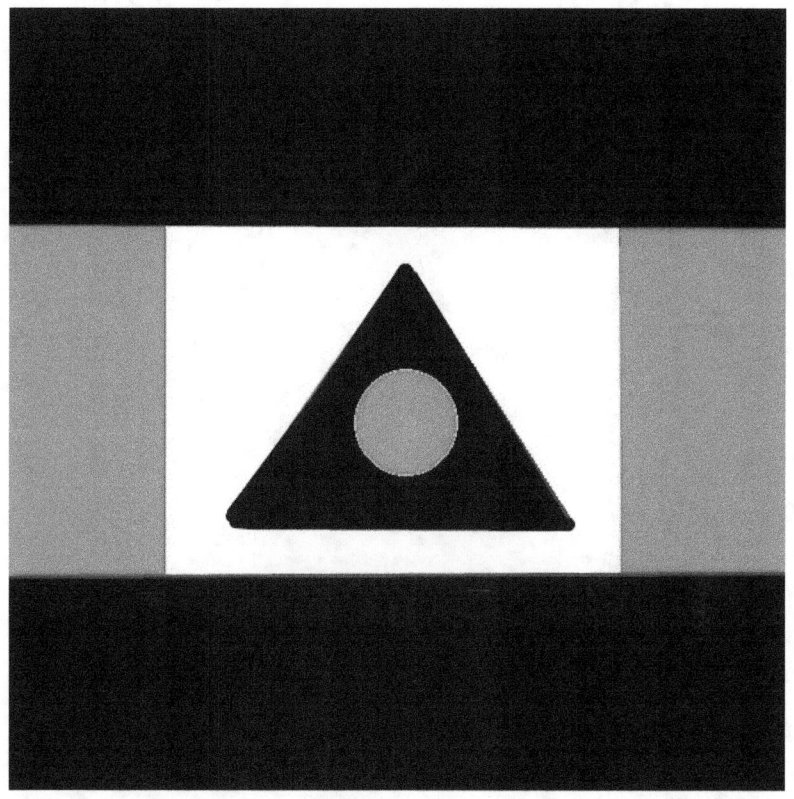

-Founded on April 22 nd, 2016-

*The Enlightened
Party Manifesto
(Its Principles &
Ideologies)*

The Enlightened
Party Manifesto
(Its Principles &
Ideologies)